What Would You Do If There Was Nothing You Had To Do?

*Practices to Create Your Life
the Way You Want It to Be*

Winslow Eliot

WHAT WOULD YOU DO IF THERE WAS NOTHING YOU HAD TO DO?

Cover design and photo: Jefferson Eliot
http://www.jasperlark.com

Author website: Tom Stier
http://www.tomstier.com

Visit the author website:
http://www.winsloweliot.com

ISBN: 978-0-9857184-5-9 (ebook)
ISBN: 978-0-9857184-6-6 (paperback)

Published by: Writespa Press
http://www.writespa.com

Acknowledgments

With enormous gratitude and love to my wise mother.

*Also, to Sheilaa Hite and her Tarot Circle: Louise Rossi,
Ralston Edwards, Ginny Guenette, Linda Farmer, Robin Hare,
and many others we met, parted from, and merrily met again.*

*Nancy Crompton, May Paddock, and Samantha Stier
for always being willing readers and exceptional editors.
Jefferson Eliot for the cover design that felt just right.*

My many students over the years, who are also my best teachers.

*And to all my teachers, past, present, future. I honor
you and am so grateful to you! I am especially grateful
to Vanelle Maunalei Love who inspired this book.*

Tracey Brennan for the "Practice, Listen, and Improvise" concept.

Claudia Jackson, John Locke, and Tom Stier, always.

What Would You Do If There Was Nothing You Had To Do?

Practices to Create Your Life
The Way You Want It to Be

THE LADY'S DAD

DEC 2012

Contents

People travel to wonder at the height of mountains, at the huge waves of the sea, at the long courses of rivers, at the vast compass of the ocean, at the circular motion of the stars; and they pass themselves by without wondering.
—St. Augustine

Foreword

What would you do if there was nothing you had to do?

Would you take the express, or the local?

Would you order coffee to go, or grind the beans yourself and enjoy the fragrance of fresh coffee wafting through the house and onto the terrace?

Would you set off on an adventure into the unknown or would you wander slowly to the hammock to rest?

What would *you* do if there was nothing you had to do?

In order to be able to answer that question, you have to know your heart's desire. That knowing may be a harder task than it first seems. Often it's easier to go about daily tasks and meet scheduled obligations than it is to know what you really want.

If you are ready to go on a path of self-discovery, to learn what your authentic self is truly asking of you in this life, then here's your opportunity. This book shows you how.

You don't have to give up anything in order to find out what you really want out of life. This is an inward journey, and it may have little to do with quitting your job, leaving your spouse, or spending less time with your children. You are going to travel a road that, as the Sufis say, is *in* the world but not *of* the world. This journey will take you through a deeply personal process so that you emerge into your 'real' world in a spirit of mindful self-creation and joy.

The mystic and psychologist Carl G. Jung called this process "individuation." Others refer to it as self-actualization, self-integration, or "finding yourself."

Know thyself and know the world, was the ancient Greek adage. You cannot truly know what your soul needs you to be doing in the world unless you "know yourself."

If you expect this to be an easy journey, think again. It's *work.* This path from where you are now through surrender through nothingness to joy is one of the hardest anyone undertakes. Usually we're forced into it, through life's experiences, challenges, tragedy, or change.

I'm offering a short cut.

I'm offering a way that transforms the work into *play.*

What would it be like to wake up with nothing to do? Imagine the birds are singing outside your window, and the garden is filled with dawn. Your house is pristine. Your mate—if you have or want one—is content. Your coffers are full, so you don't have to earn money today. Your children or other relatives are happy. Your parents don't need you. Your friends are fine. You are care-free. You have no responsibilities, obligations, duties, shoulds, have-tos, musts ... *Nothing* you have to do.

There's only you, just beautiful you, in the universe.

What would you choose to do with you—*just you?*

Maybe you'd re-read a beloved novel?

Maybe have a long bath scented with rosemary?

Take a walk?

Do you long to talk with someone or are you glad of the silence?

Would you call a friend because the loneliness is a bit scary?

Do you prefer to lie in bed and daydream, or do you jump up, eager for an activity, greeting the day with energy and action?

How do you know what kind of person you really are, what your soul thirsts for, if you don't give it a chance to find out?

Most of our lives are measured out in coffee spoons—meaning we wake up, brush our teeth, have our coffee, go to work, recover from the day, then it's time for dinner, time to go to bed ... there's family-and-friend time in there, and, if you're lucky, perhaps a vacation—which means vacation from work. And, typically, vacations are not excellent opportunities to find yourself. When you wake up in a strange hotel room or sip a margarita by the pool, you're recovering from work, not finding your inner peace. You're saying to yourself, *I'm so glad I'm here— what a relief—it's snowing up north ... nice getaway.*

So I'm wondering this: why would you *want* to get away from your daily life?

When I first began telling people that I was writing this book, the response was typically startled surprise. The immediate interest, curiosity, and the intense longing for a map to this kind of self-discovery were palpable. One young woman asked urgently, "Do you *know?*"

I responded by saying, "I know how to help *you* to know. That's what my book is about."

Only you have your own answers. I'm giving you a map, a compass, and solid walking shoes. The map is your powerful mind; your compass is your authentic feeling-nature. The shoes are your physical body and the time and space in which you live.

Most importantly, I'm giving you twenty-two keys that will open twenty-two doors, each one going deeper into discovering your heart's desire.

If you do the practices I outline in this book, and accept the process taking as long as it needs to take, I believe you will find out not only what you would do if there was nothing you had to do, but who you really are and your soul's purpose.

Choose the freedom of now. For you are not your mind or your memories or thought-pictures that torment you. You are an undying spirit that can be fanned like a fire and renewed. —Kristin Zambucka

If one advances confidently in the direction of his dreams, and endeavors to live the life which he has imagined, he will meet with a success unexpected in common hours. –Henry David Thoreau

Introduction

We all experience turning points in our lives, sometimes several times in a decade or even within a year. My biggest turning point took place in Hawai'i. I was offered a position at the Honolulu Waldorf School, I grabbed my good-natured children and reluctant husband, and we left Massachusetts behind.

Around my fiftieth birthday, on the island of O'ahu, I met a wise woman called Vanelle Maunalei Love. I told her I had visited all the sacred places on as many islands as I could, I said I had read pretty much everything Maxwell Freedom Long and others had written about Hawaiian huna, the ancient sacred teachings of the Pacific islanders. I was in the process of learning the magical language, which I had discovered was at the heart of huna. I was also taking hula dance lessons, that I understood as much as I could about ancient Hawaiian mysticism, but that I had not been able to penetrate its essence.

To be honest, I did not think she could help me. In all my spiritual seeking, I had not yet found a teacher or guide who did not toss my earnest seeking back into my lap and tell me to find out for myself. I appreciated all those teachers for the faith they had in me to do just that, but still I longed for one who would really open a door for me in some way.

With polite enthusiasm and inner skepticism, I agreed to accompany Maunalei on an expedition to some of Oʻahu's sacred places where she generously offered to share what she could.

This is what happened: We drove along the Pali to one of the most famous tourist look-out points on Oʻahu: where Kamehameha fought a crucial battle in his task of unifying all the Hawaiian islands two centuries ago. The place was swarming with busloads of tourists, the air was filled with the chatter of dozens of foreign languages, and the relentless clicks of cameras and iPhones. My heart sank—I did not want to hear again about Kamehameha's victory, at the cost of so many lives of men, the men who fell off the edge of that high, windy cliff. It is said that sometimes you can still hear the shrieks of the dying soldiers as they plummeted 300 feet to their doom.

It's also said that on windy days you can lean over the cliff and balance against the wind, and some have died that way, too.

But Maunalei told me that the place was much more than a historical site. It had a sacred energy all its own, completely apart from politics, tragedy, or foolhardiness.

I followed docilely through the exhaust fumes near the stairs leading to the lookout. There, Maunalei paused and said quietly, "This is where we need to chant an ʻoli to let the spirit of the ʻaina know we are visiting with respect for the area. We are asking to be welcomed. We are also acknowledging who we are and letting them know our intentions are pono."

And, standing with a matter-of-fact inward stillness, oblivious to the people swarming around us, she began to chant quietly in Hawaiian.

As she chanted the strangest thing happened. Everything around us grew quiet, except for her low voice. I couldn't hear the chatter, the camera clicks, footsteps—*nothing*. I could still see the people, but they seemed in a different dimension. They were as innocuous as lovely flowers. That was it: I felt I was in a meadow of lovely flowers—but I couldn't hear them or communicate with them in any way. Maunalei and I were completely alone, there on the cliff top, outside the realm of space or time.

I blinked, thinking I could revert back to my more familiar dimension, but it would not come. She and I were still isolated.

What is fascinating about the power of "knowing" is that you can't tell someone else what you know and expect them to get it. It has to be your own experience. I can repeat, word for word, what Maunalei told me after she had finished chanting and took me along some dirt paths beyond the lookout point, and the answers she gave to my many questions, but unless you were there, in her presence, high up on the Pali, in another dimension, they remain just concepts.

But what I *can* share with you is how you, too, can come to that same "knowing" in your own life.

Because when Maunalei spoke, everything fell into place for me: I knew that I *really* could create my own reality.

&—

Also, I can tell you a little about Hawaiian mysticism.

Hawaiian spirituality is based on a complicated and rich ten-fold view of the human being. The three basic aspects of each of us are our thinking, feeling, and physical natures. Each of these is divided into three parts, which creates a nine-fold human being. The tenth being is the integration of all the others.

Here's a description of how the ancient Hawaiians viewed your thinking self or mind:

Like many of our modern-day psychologists, ancient Hawaiians believed that human beings have three 'minds': the rational mind, the subconscious/ unconscious mind, and spirit or higher-self mind.

Hawaiians called those three minds your three spirits, and your task in life is to integrate them, so each can nurture and care for each other. The first mind is called the *uhane,* which is your rational mind. Like the ancient Egyptians, who carefully preserved every single organ after death as being important in the afterlife, but tossed out the brain as no longer being necessary, the Hawaiians regarded the brain as an excellent tool for your time on this physical plane, but not at all useful in the spiritual world. Westerners often confuse the mind with the real 'you'—as though by looking out of your eyes from your brain, you *are* your brain.

According to the Ancient Hawaiians, this is not so.

Then there is your *unihipili,* or your subconscious/unconscious part, which Max Freedom Long translates (each syllable has various meanings in the Hawaiian language) thus: "A spirit which can grieve but may not be able to talk; something that covers up something else and hides it, or is itself hidden as by a cover or veil; a spirit which accompanies another, is joined to it, is sticky, and sticks or adheres to it. It attaches itself to another and acts as its servant; it is a spirit which does things secretly, silently, and very carefully, but does not do certain things because it is afraid of offending the gods; it is a spirit that can protrude from something, can rise up from that something, and which can also draw something out of something, as a coin from a pocket. It desires things mostly earnestly. It is stubborn and unwilling, disposed to refuse to do as told. It tinctures or impregnates or mixes completely with something else."

Your unihipili can also be related to your astral or soul body. In the Christian mystical tradition the soul is a still, small quiet voice within, a voice obscured by the relentless noise of the rational mind. One of the definitions of unihipili is "a grasshopper" and when I first heard that I was immediately reminded of Pinocchio's conscience: Jiminy Cricket or your "cricket on the hearth." Your conscience is that rare place where reason and feeling meet to create a sense of well-being, simply because you have done the right thing. (Literally, the word conscience means "innermost thoughts, desires, intentions;

feelings" and also "knowledge within oneself, sense of right, a moral sense.")

The Hawaiians called the higher self the *aumakua*. Although a literal translation is your deified family ancestor, or the wise, loving parents who take care of you, the spirit of an aumakua is closer to Jung's concept of archetype, collective unconscious, or folk soul.

In Hawaiian mysticism, your brain or mental self cannot reach your higher self (aumakua) without going through your unihipili or feeling self. Your unihipili is not a pot of roiling suppressed fears, base instincts, and out-of-control emotions, as Freud might have us believe, but a wise and caring friend who aids you on your path toward self-integration. That integration of all your selves—or spirits—is essential to your well-being and inner peace.

This is your inner voice—and you have to learn to listen to it if you are to find out what you really want to be doing with your life.

To go back to the idea of the nine-fold human being, made up of mind, body, and soul: the ancient Hawaiians regarded spiritual development as the literal creation and growth of a fourth body as a part of your total human beingness. This fourth body was sometimes referred to also as the aumakua or the "kino kupanaha," meaning the strange or wondrous body. In the esoteric path of anthroposophy this development can be seen as the incarnation of the ego—the sensitive growth of a person's physical, etheric, astral bodies that throughout childhood prepare a human being for the development of their self or ego.

The point is that each of us is born and as we grow we undergo a maturation process in all parts of ourselves. Only when we are more integrated within ourselves do we have the foundation and the freedom truly to become our "strange and wondrous selves." The alchemists believed that that path of transmutation leads to immortality—and that is the truth: for no matter what your belief system, our consciousness is made up of an eternal alloy of freedom and love.

That's the experience we all long for.

That's the experience you are headed for on this journey.

Practice, Listen, and Improvise

Each of the twenty-two stages of your journey is divided into two parts. The first part describes where you are on the journey and gives you the whys and the wherefores. The second part offers exercises for you to work with for as long as you want or need to before moving on to the next phase of your journey. These exercises are based on Practicing, Listening, and Improvising.

The nature of all human endeavor is threefold. First, we feel or desire, then we strategize a way of fulfilling that desire, then we act on that strategy. Feeling—thinking—acting.

Sometimes, we're going to break up the pattern in the exercise process. First you'll act—you'll activate your will. You'll have the opportunity to do things not because you want to or because you think it's a good idea, but because the exercise of 'doing' is what shakes up the status quo and furthers your development. It also strengthens your will power and helps you to see how you can change things in your life.

By "listening" I mean listening to yourself. What you feel about the experience of the exercises is essential to finding out what you would do if there was nothing you had to do. Your emotional life—not your stuck-in-the-past or I'm-scared emotions, but your powerful inner compass that urges you to speak to that person or turn left up ahead, and that you usually squash with a ferocious mental energy of 'reason'—is crucial to this journey. *Listen to your feelings.*

Here's something you need to know about listening—something you can make use of in your relationships as well as when you listen to yourself: *Listening is a practice in and of itself.* When I suggest you write down your experience and what you feel about it, in other words to listen to yourself, that's all you need to do. Just as when a friend complains about a co-worker or moans about the heat, she's not necessarily asking you to get her co-worker fired or to get some ice-cubes. She just wants you to listen. Don't judge, don't solve, don't opine. Simply listen.

Listen to yourself in the same way.

By "improvise" I mean thinking outside the box. Your mind is much more flexible and imaginative than you typically allow it to be. We all get caught up in dogma, prejudice, concepts, what we've been taught, and what we think is right. We mostly stop flexing our mental muscles to incorporate the vastness of the improbable or what we might fear is impossible. In order to create the reality you want, you need to strengthen and stretch your mental powers so that they're supple, lithe, strong, and friendly. Improvising is a great way to do this.

What you need to bring with you:

Essential:

- A journal. This journal is for you, and for you alone. It's essential, because by writing your intentions and your experiences, you'll see where you've come from and where you're going. It's human nature to have a memory *and* a sense of where you're headed. By writing your experience, you're placing yourself in the present, right in the stream of life, like a rock over which a river flows and sparkles, bends, and twirls. Choose a time to write in your journal that's as consistent as possible. Either first thing in the morning or last thing at night probably works best, but you decide. What matters is that you write in it every day, and that you do it at more or less the same time every day.

Recommended:

- A jump rope.
- Juggling balls or three bean bags.
- A token or ring.

- A pendulum.
- A seashell in which you can hear the ocean.
- A place to be alone.
- Something exquisite to smell, taste, and touch.
- An empty box.
- A calendar of the phases of the moon.
- An open mind.

Enough words have been exchanged; now at last let me see some deeds!
                                                              –Goethe

0. Beginning: *Where do I start?*

There are two mistakes one can make along the road to truth:
not going all the way, and not starting. –Buddha

How do you begin?

Here's the first thing you have to know:

Start where you are.

This is true of every journey.

I've taken so many journeys in my life, sometimes it takes my breath away to think of it. When I was two, my parents moved from my birth city of New York to Spain, when my father received a Guggenheim fellowship to write a book. While they were there, they traveled to Greece and visited Delphi, and decided there was no better place to raise children. So we lived in the mountains near Olympus for a few years, until my mother decided my brother and I were ready to learn some geography, and the best way to do that would be to take a round-the-world trip on a freighter.

There are so many kinds of journeys, not just the geographical ones that I became so familiar with. There are the journeys of friendships, of love affairs, of raising children, of careers, of creating a home. Education is a journey—and a hobby or avocation can be a journey, if you allow it to.

Each time you set off, you're trusting in the unknown. You're bundling up what matters most to you, leaving the rest behind, and taking a step off the edge of a cliff.

Start where you are.

Whether you're in a powerful emotional upheaval in your life, or you've finally found the peace and space you need to undertake this process, start where you are. Nothing will be gained by leaping ahead, or believing in something you're not ready for, or risking something that will lead to regret if it's lost.

Take small steps. Baby steps. Feel your way. Learn to trust yourself as you head out: you'll discover that you're far wiser, far more capable, and far braver than you ever dreamed.

Since you're reading this book, *you are ready* to take a small step that will change your life. You've already taken the first step. You've taken the risk of accepting the fact that you want to know yourself—to find your authentic self.

Because that's what this book is about. What would you do if there was nothing you had to do? Who are you, really?

Your journey through this book and the practices it offers is what many might call the Fool's journey. In our hearts, we're all Fools. We don't have a clue, really, about how to live. We are given—to a greater or lesser extent—guidelines from our parents and teachers, and we hope those role models show us the way of kindness, competence, and confidence to meet the world and our destinies.

But there comes a time in life when we all meet something we have no tools for. We really don't know what it's going to be like when the love of our life decides he or she likes someone more than us. We've heard the songs, watched the movies—and *still* we have no idea.

We have no idea how to be a parent either. Only by stepping off the cliff into the uncharted world of 'family' do we learn that raising children is not a skill but an experience.

Here's another one: Very few people are prepared to die. And yet dying happens to us all. It's the ultimate stepping off the cliff into the cloud of unknowing.

This book is not going to tell you how to raise children or have a great relationship or die gracefully. But it will show you how to discover who *you* are, as a full, deep, rounded human being, which includes your greatness and your shadow, so that you can live the life that actualizes and fulfills you as you are meant to be.

You are the wise fool—the holy fool. Just by virtue of the fact you were born, this is so. You've agreed to step out onto a ledge and be born into a world that is unfamiliar and live a destiny about which you don't have a clue. You're excited, brave, and perhaps nervous. Or maybe your parents or teachers made you feel nervous, and you seek an essential equanimity and calm. Or perhaps you're brave and impulsive, and you'll discover latent qualities of introspection and stillness.

Being a Fool doesn't have to be scary—it's exciting. You are eager, adventurous, longing to succeed, and longing to be free of constraints. It's not easy to shed these. "You must!" "You should!" are heard all the time, from the time we're babies. "Don't do that!" "You don't want that!" "Be nice!" "Be careful!" "Be good!" "Don't go that way!"

By undertaking this journey, you've made a pact with yourself to put aside—at least in your mind and for a time—all the shoulds and don'ts and musts by which you live your life. It's okay if your outfit isn't ideal or your shoes have holes. Nothing matters except the will to set out. It's not always easy, and it's a delicate time—the tenderest awakening from a cocoon of safety to hard-earned insight and experience. In order to know the world, you must know yourself.

Learning to know *you* can be tumultuous, delicate, brave, emotional.

You've already begun.

What you're going to find out is that there is not just one cliff out there: you're going to step over the edges of cliff after cliff in this process.

Your cliff is your heart's desire. Step close to the edge. You have nothing else to do. Nowhere else to go. *What would you do?*

Step over the edge.

You're falling.

Yes, that's what happens when you step over the edge of a cliff: *You begin to fall.*

Luckily, it's a long way down, and as you drop, perhaps terrified, into a new way of existence, you discover something marvelous:

You're not falling! You're flying!

Now what?

> *Come to the edge, He said.*
> *They said: We are afraid.*
> *Come to the edge, He said.*
> *They came. He pushed them,*
> *And they flew . . ."*

– *Guillaume Apollinaire*

Practice, Improvise, Listen

Practice: *Leaping*

Your first practice in this journey is easy.

Leap.

Jump. Hop.

Use a jump rope or a trampoline or jump up and down on your bed.

Leap across a stream, or hop onto the sidewalk, or up the stairs. Grow conscious of the motion of leaping in your everyday life. If you're confined to a wheelchair or your legs are frail, you can still do this exercise. Lift your arms and really feel them lighten. Practice even wiggling each finger so that it feels lighter.

Using your imagination, imbue your limbs and organs with light. It's not a coincidence that the word 'light' is used to describe illumination *and* being light as a feather.

Imagine you are a frog. Frogs could not leap as high as they do without springs in their legs. Imagine your leg muscle shortening like a frog's, loading energy into your tendons, then recoiling like a spring to propel you high up into the sky. Simply imagining the process will give you a feeling of elasticity and ease.

By physically growing conscious of your body as being equal parts levity and gravity, you'll immediately start to feel more balance and potentiality in your life. We tend to be much more connected and seduced by gravity. Gravity makes your leap off a cliff a trip with an itinerary to the ground rather than a leap of faith into freedom. You are much more weighed down by your mass than lifted by your weightlessness. Gravity is solid, heavy, substantive.

Levity is the opposite of gravity, and yet is hardly ever taken seriously. (The reverse—it's usually taken to mean 'a joke.') Levity is weightlessness.

Gravity is sometimes described as an attraction between two bodies but, more correctly, gravity strives to reach a center. It's less attraction (which is magnetism) and more like *contraction*. It exists in *space*. Like light, levity exists in *time* and moves like light: *it expands outward.*

You need both to exist, but it is easier to be aware of gravity. Levity needs to be brought to consciousness.

Begin your journey by shaking things up a bit and become aware of your lightness of being. Leap as often as you can.

Listen: *Journaling*

In your journal, write down what you feel when you leap or jump up and down or try to jump rope.

Silly? Dizzy? Sweaty? Foolish? Exhilarated?

Here's something you need to know about writing in your journal. Some people find it fairly easy to write, others find it harder.

Here are some guidelines to help you with your flow:

First of all, don't self-edit. No one cares if you spell correctly, punctuate, or have a dramatic opening sentence. Rather, write in a stream-of-consciousness. You don't even need to use full sentences.

Really loosen up: Write in your journal upside-down sometimes, or put one word on each line, or create a symbol with your words on the page, like a square or a circle. Perhaps you want to paste in a leaf or a seed. Or use colored pencils.

In this process of 'listening' to your feelings about leaping and jumping, you are bringing to the forefront of your consciousness the qualities of levity in your life. What makes you feel light, expansive?

The streams of images, thoughts, and emotions that flow when you record your emotional response to your practice are not mere fragments of words and scribbles. They are a record of your *listening* to yourself.

Honor them. Have fun with them. Play with them.

Improvise: *Do something new*

Now do something every day that you have never done before. This may be as small as having tea instead of coffee in the morning, or going somewhere you have never been. If you've never had a pedicure, try it out. Walked into a store that's way beyond your means? Told a friend you love her?

Intention is essential in all the practices I give here, so write down what you intend to do each day that is entirely new and different.

When you take your walk, head in the opposite direction.

If you dress before breakfast, this time dress afterward.

Shake things up.

This practice might seem small, but you'll find that taking baby steps into the unknown will make a huge difference toward reaching your goal.

Action is good, but there are other ways you can shake things up. Don't just *do* something new, try *thinking* differently.

Think outside your comfort zone. Imagine something you can't imagine. Look down at the sky. Open a box from the inside.

Here's an example from an interview with the novelist Toni Morrison (*The Guardian*, April 13, 2012).

When Morrison was 17, she had tried out a thought experiment. On the news, she had seen footage of some white mothers in the south trying to turn over a school bus with black children in it. "I didn't know if I could turn over a bus full of little white kids. I didn't know if I could feel that... fury. And I tried very hard to. This is what I did: I said suppose... horses began to speak. And began to demand their rights. Now, I've ridden horses. They're very good workers. They're very good racehorses. Suppose they just... want more. Suppose they want to go to school! Suppose they want to sit next to me in the theatre. I began to feel this sense of—'I like you, but...'; 'You're good, but...' Suppose they want to sleep with my children?!" She's laughing heartily now. *"I had to go outside the species! But it worked, I could feel it. You know; don't sit next to me."*

It's even harder to *feel* something you've never felt before than it is to think a new thought. But your thoughts can actually impact your feelings, if you practice.

Try to imagine yourself as a stone, or a flower. Or imagine a political or religious thought antithetical to yours and find something about it that you can sit with.

By leaving behind the relative safety of what you know, you will make it impossible to go back to the person you were before. As you unlock the rest of the doors to discovering what and who you really are, come back to this chapter and remind yourself of these first steps you took.

What a wonderful life I've had! I only wish I'd realized it sooner. —Colette

Part 1—Thinking

At the still point of the turning world. Neither flesh nor fleshless;
Neither from nor towards; at the still point, there the dance is,
But neither arrest nor movement. And do not call it fixity,
Where past and future are gathered. Neither movement from nor towards,
Neither ascent nor decline. Except for the point, the still point,
There would be no dance, and there is only the dance,
I can only say, there we have been: but I cannot say where.
And I cannot say, how long, for that is to place it in time.
The inner freedom from the practical desire,
The release from action and suffering, release from the inner
And the outer compulsion, yet surrounded
By a grace of sense, a white light still and moving.
                                    –T. S. Eliot, from *The Four Quartets*

1. Flowing: *The art of effortless concentration*

There are infinite realms of possibility in your life. You *can* do anything. You *can* do everything.

In this chapter I'll show you how your energy can meet

opportunity and conspire with your growing intuition to create the reality you desire.

It's only the false magician inside you that creates the illusion that you're at the mercy of circumstance or society. You actually don't "have to" do anything you don't want to. Something stops you from building a house, or running away, or quitting a job. Perhaps it's your conscience, or a feeling of guilt or responsibility, or your plans for the future, or financial constraints.

But you *can* change anything you choose. The consequences may not be what you'd like, but you can do it. Anything. Right now. Today.

Many years ago I had a fabulous job at a magazine in New York City. The pay was more than I'd imagined I'd ever make, the expense account mind-boggling, and the benefits (including a splendid pension plan) superb. I was being 'groomed' to go far in the company—I could tell, because I was treated with kid gloves (or, as I chose to call them, "golden handcuffs").

I was on my way to the lifestyle and career I'd strived for. Then why did I feel so ... *confused?*

There I was, a young woman, with my own Greenwich Village apartment, working in publishing (my passion), making plenty of money, partying with friends I cared about, hanging out with an ideal boyfriend, plenty of hobbies ... and yet I dreaded my Monday through Friday, nine-in-the-morning to very-late-at-night, work week.

One night I had a dream. I was in a castle and I didn't know how to get out. The castle was huge, set high up on a hill. The stone walls were thick and safe, so there was no way we could be attacked by enemies. The spiral stairs, as I mounted them to a tower, felt as solid as a mountain.

And then I heard a voice. It was so piercingly clear it seemed to come from the stones themselves.

Get out!

Terrified, I fled toward a narrow window, thinking I could jump, but a strange metal sheet, acting like a portcullis, crashed down just as I reached it, leaving the small room in twilight. Panicking, I fled down the stairs, but the metal door at the bottom clanged impenetrably shut as well.

I looked around. All the doors and windows were closing down, leaving me in increasing darkness. I was so afraid I thought I would faint.

Then I heard the voice again. *You can get out. There is a way out. But it's a magic way. It's not forcing your way out with an axe or trying to send a message for help to an army on the outside. That won't work. It's another way entirely.*

I had the dream in late August, and forgot about it until sometime in October when it resurfaced with the force of the clanging sound of the metal doors. The solution to my confusion and dread was so simple, so obvious, that it seemed incredible I had not realized it before.

I could quit.

Now you may have already realized that it was obvious I could quit my job. But when you're in the throes of your early career, and you have everything you've worked hard for finally come to fruition, and you're independent so you absolutely *need* the income... well, it may not occur to you that that's an option.

It had not occurred to me that I could leave what appeared to be the perfect job.

Until that dream fermented in my unconscious and reemerged as a sparkling wine—reminding me that I was a free agent, that I had a life to live, that if I was wasting that much time doing something I did not love doing I was going to get farther and farther off track from my life's purpose, not closer—until that happened, I thoroughly believed I had to stay where I was. I didn't even see I had a choice!

When I gave my notice there was an outcry from practically everyone I knew. My connection in the personnel department

33

was particularly upset. She even offered to sweeten my pension plan.

Pension? I was in my early twenties, and although I was told we really need to plan ahead, it just did not seem worth it. Why put off happiness and enjoyment till retirement? Besides, I had the powerful vision of spending my whole life in a thickly-walled stone room in a castle, with solid metal sheathing the windows and doors. Did I really want to spend the next forty years inside?

I gratefully but firmly refused to stay.

I'm not telling you to quit your job if you don't like it. I'm telling you that you *can* quit. Then, if you decide you don't want to, you realize that you're staying on out of your own free will, not because the doors and windows are locked.

You may weigh the consequences of leaving a relationship, a house, or a job and decide that, actually, looking at it from every angle, you'd really prefer to stay where you are. Retirement *is* an issue to consider. But the actual practice of imagining yourself free of something you thought you were stuck in will move you closer to your goal: discovering what you would do if there was nothing you *had* to do.

For me, the decision to quit made me realize that I wanted to be a writer. Every job, relationship, or living situation was going to have to support my writing in some way. But I did not realize my passion until I stepped off the chariot that was taking me in another direction.

So what's your next step?

In order to create the universe of your dreams you need to

- have an imagination
- project that imagination (create an intention)
- take action—do it.

That's what it takes: Imagination—Projection—Action.

Your *imagination* is inspired by your feeling or intuition. Sometimes it shows up as longing or desire.

Projection is how you analyze the hows, whens, and wheres. You figure out the possibilities.

Then you take *action*.

Okay, but what if you don't have an image of what to do? I had not a clue where to go or how to move on when I was stuck at an unfulfilling job. Nothing seemed better than where I was.

You don't have to know the answer to that yet. Creating the initial imagination of how you'd like your daily life to be is not as easy as it might seem. You might imagine you'd love to be by a swimming pool somewhere in Mexico, but the heat, the margaritas, and the leisure might pall after a while.

Or maybe it wouldn't.

So how do you decide what it is you want to do?

Start by imagining the *feeling* you want to have—not the activity itself. For example, do you want a sense of tranquility in your life, or adventure, or passion? Don't get specific about the 'hows'—focus on the ideal feeling.

However it manifests to you personally, in your life, describe your feeling of satisfaction and well-being. Imagine it with the same thrill as the feeling of falling freshly in love.

Imagine being absolutely connected with what you're doing and where you are.

In his book called *Flow*, Mihaly Csikszentmihalyi describes being so involved in an activity that nothing else seems to matter: "The experience itself is so enjoyable that people will do it even at great cost, for the sheer sake of doing it."

At this point in your journey it doesn't matter *what* you do to get that awe-inspiring feeling of "flow"—what matters is that you experience it.

Later, you can recognize it in the future as a state of being that you enjoy and discover your way of getting there.

Acquiring the feeling of "flow" is not a magic trick (although it sometimes may seem like it) nor is it the purview solely of artists or inventors. Here are some ways you can bring the experience of 'flow' into your own life:

Learn a challenging activity that requires practice and skill. Choose something that isn't so difficult that you're anxious, nor so easy that you become bored.

Set small, attainable goals toward mastering your new skill and celebrate each time one of those goals is met.

Concentrate on the activity. If your mind wanders, bring it gently back to the task on hand. Don't be hard on yourself for becoming distracted. Just let any anxiety or self-doubt drift through you and disappear. Focus on what you're doing.

As your skill improves, you'll feel a growing sense of being in control. According to Csikszentmihalyi, it's not being in control that matters so much as your feeling that you can exercise control when you're confronted by more challenging situations.

As you progress, you'll lose your self-consciousness. This is the famous stage in which you merge with the activity you're doing. You become "completely involved in an activity for its own sake. The ego falls away. Time flies. Every action, movement, and thought follows inevitably from the previous one, like playing jazz. Your whole being is involved, and you're using your skills to the utmost."

When this happens, your sense of time is altered: Seconds may seem like hours. Hours might seem like the blink of an eye.

This process brings you to an ideal state of effortless concentration. For a pianist, the effortless concentration comes from thousands of hours of practicing scales over and over, until his fingers are one with the piano. It's then that he can freely play.

The poet Robert Frost wrote "Stopping by the Woods on a Snowy Evening" after having stayed up one summer night writing ("practicing") a long—and forgettable—poem called "New Hampshire." Exhausted, he went outside and saw the sun rising, and was suddenly inspired to write a poem "about the snowy evening and the little horse as if I'd had a hallucination in just a few minutes without strain."

The experience of 'flow' is like swimming hard under water, and then breaking through the surface to the air and floating on your back.

You need to become so involved in something that it becomes you.

You learn to see by practice. It's just like playing tennis, you get better the more you play. The more you look around at things, the more you see. The more you photograph, the more you realize what can be photographed and what can't be photographed. You just have to keep doing it. –Eliot Porter

Practice, Listen, and Improvise

Practice: *Learn to juggle.*

Yes, that's right. Get out your beanbags or juggling balls and juggle.

Start with just one ball and toss it gently from one hand to the other, back and forth. Then use two.

You might be surprised how easy it is.

When you feel ready, bring out your third ball or beanbag. The trick to becoming good is not to pass one of the balls from one hand to the other, but to toss it also in the air, so there are two balls being tossed at the same time. This takes some confidence and a lot of practice, but you'll get better faster if you follow the instructions that come with your juggling balls.

Watch how a juggler juggles: There seems to be no effort to his dance, pleasure, and one-ness with his beanbags or juggling balls. It's transforming work into play, which is part of the secret of flow.

Schedule between ten minutes and one hour for this activity every day. Close the door, turn off the phone, set a timer, and don't allow any interruptions. Juggle the whole time you've set for yourself, even if you get frustrated by your ineptness.

The important thing is to focus as completely as possible on the activity, and to let your mind and body learn to be effortlessly connected to it. The way you learn this seemingly impossible task is through transposing your brain's instructions to the rhythmic system; from your mind and imagination to that of your will power. That is why the word 'practice' is so important. You need to practice over and over, whether you're juggling or loving or living.

You want to get to the point where juggling is as effortless as breathing or walking. You'll find yourself free to move in and out of this zone, not just when you're concentrating on juggling, but when you're involved in any activity.

Effortless activity.

In Taoism there is a similar concept called "wu wei" which can be translated as "non-doing," "non-action" or "the action of non-action."

Juggling reminds you that there's no separation between mind and body, and the energy that is released is indeed effortless. We tend to listen far too much to the incessant chatter of our minds, and that can create frustration and blockage. Juggling shows us that work—concentrating on accomplishing something—can be transformed into play when it flows.

Because when you're in the flow, it's all one.

Listen: *Keep doing it*

Runners and swimmers experience flow regularly. Artists experience it too. In fact, we've all experienced this. Even if, in the past, you felt it was some sort of grace or endorphins or luck, now is your opportunity to realize that you can create this experience of flow for yourself, simply through practice.

A juggler juggles effortlessly. You can see it in his grace, his smile, his skill. His focus seems effortless—but it has taken years of practice to get to this effortlessness.

It may seem paradoxical that so much concentration on tuning in to your inner voice could create effortlessness—but that's not the case. Think of it this way: Practice is essential to everything we do. It's part of the path of apprenticeship. An artist paints the same still life over and over or experiments with the same color. A great chef starts his career by slicing carrots, lots of carrots. When he finally is declared a master it is because he effortlessly slices those carrots into transparent disks. The pianist effortlessly plays the moonlight sonata. A poem effortlessly pours from the soul of a poet.

The effortlessness comes after hard work, study, focus, knowledge, and dedication.

It comes *because* of the effort.

Let your mind and body be carried by the rhythm and movement of the juggling balls. Let your breathing breathe itself, let your body move by itself. Focus intently, until you no longer have to focus.

Pay attention not just to your breathing and your thoughts, but to your emotional state. Learning to juggle can be frustrating, just as the beginning of learning any skill can be difficult. But with regular practice you'll reach that remarkable breakthrough where you're one with the act, and the flow comes. Work becomes play.

Effortless concentration shows you how your work can become play.

The more often you do this, the more you'll realize that you are free.

Free to do what you want to do.

Even if you don't yet know what that is.

If you do this as steadily and strongly as possible, an interesting thing begins to happen. You're not breathing—you become the breath. When you're writing about your experience you're no longer the writer, but simply the scribe. The words come through you.

Ultimately, your effort is to be one with being human, and one with the divine, and allowing both these aspects of yourself to become still, deep within your soul. In that silence, you can begin to create the magic that is to become the life you long for.

Improvise: *Have fun*

Smile. Smile as you juggle. Intentionally smiling can boost your mood: Psychologists have found that even if you're in bad mood, you can instantly lift your spirits by forcing yourself to smile. Somehow, your smile-muscles send a memo to your obedient brain, telling it you're feeling cheerful. In response, your brain releases happiness hormones like endorphins that really do cheer you.

Your physical muscles override your mood.

Also, it's easier to smile than to frown, so if you're frowning with concentration, you're adding to your strain. Like walking, smiling is an innate aspect of being human, it's not a learned function, like behavior. Even blind babies smile. Humans *need* to smile. So smile while you juggle.

Be inventive: Vary your pattern, throw a ball or beanbag higher than you think you can. When you do this, look out at an imaginary audience and take a bow while the ball is still in the air.

Try juggling as you're walking backward or standing on a chair or jumping up and down on a trampoline.

Try juggling something different: how about sticks, apples, oranges, scarves, pinecones ... choose something fun.

Try juggling with a blindfold on.

Okay, if juggling just really isn't your thing, choose something else. How about hula hoop? Or mastering the yo-yo?

Or my favorite: whirling like a dervish. Find some sublime Sufi music and learn to turn with the universe.

Choose something that takes just enough effort so that you can focus intensely for a certain amount of time. Your goal is to enter a state of concentration, where you are one with your inner self, your time, and your space.

In *Meditations on the Tarot*, the anonymous author gives you three tools at this stage in your journey: "Learn at first concentration without effort; transform work into play; make every yoke that you have accepted easy and every burden that you carry light."

In other words, "Seriously, have fun."

Life is like a mirror. Smile at it and it smiles back at you. —**Peace Pilgrim**

*All rational beings, angels and men, possess two faculties, the power of
knowing and the power of loving.* —From The Cloud of Unknowing

2. Knowing: *Accessing your inner voice*

I n this next phase of your journey you will become aware of
the depth and helpfulness of your unihipili, or intuitive, self.
Unless you learn to consciously relate to and communicate
with your subconscious, the thread that connects your
mind/physical existence to your spiritual, "higher" self, you'll be
stuck in a realm of separation from yourself.

Whether you are a man or a woman, for this particular stage of
the journey you are accessing the feminine side of your being.
You can't be a whole person without opposites: yin-yang, dark-
light, negative-positive, and male-female are essential to being
human. The receptive qualities are undervalued in Western
society, and both men and women suffer because of that. We

admire action, success, accomplishment, light. We tend to be afraid of the dark and we typically mistrust what we don't know.

And yet, womanly wisdom is a way of "knowing" at the essence of life.

How can you access your inner voice, the voice that senses someone's mood, the voice that comes through you when you are helping someone in need, the voice that directs you out of the forest when you're lost? And, once you access it, how do you know it's real and not made up? How can you trust it?

Your mind works in three ways:

Thinking about something—which is active (planning, analyzing, contemplating). We call that "active thinking." This requires concentration and focus.

Then there's daydreaming, which is "passive thinking." You let thoughts drift in and out and hardly pay attention to them. This requires letting go of your focus and letting your mind flow like water.

Then there is "active listening."

Active listening is the point where your conscious and unconscious meet.

I experience it as the tiny or enormous point where nature, human being, and spirit arrive at a crossroads at the same time, and converse in a mutually understandable language.

Active listening requires tuning in to a voice that is not intellectual, nor soft and daydreamy. It is as substantive and clear as the strains of music from a violin or a painting on the wall. Yet it is not experienced by ear or eye. The sound is as clear as the sound of bell or words spoken out loud, and yet they are not out loud. For instance, one morning I was awakened by the ringing of the telephone. It was a concrete ringing sound—so loud that it woke me. I waited, listening for the second ring, which did not come. As I lay in bed, I realized the sound was inside me.

You may not experience "knowing" through sound. You may experience it as a sensation in the pit of your stomach. You may feel the hairs on the back of your neck rising. Your palms might get sweaty. *Listen to your body.*

Or you may experience "knowing" through symbols in the world around you, and your response to them.

The knowing that comes to you when you are actively listening is something that is neither real nor unreal, just as a dream exists in a dimension that is outside of what we perceive to be real or unreal.

For many of us, the experience of "knowing" means a scientific-proof kind of knowing: *I know because I see and hear and touch and taste it.* For others, knowing is a leap of faith. Sometimes it's couched in a sacred or emotional longing to know the purpose for our existence. This can sometimes be confused with *believing* rather than knowing.

The knowing that comes through intuition is literally experienced. When you actively listen and turn the mental knob in your brain as though on an old-fashioned radio dial—trying to tune in to a certain frequency—there is absolutely no question that you've found the station. You'll hear mental static, you'll hear a program but it's classical music (or perhaps you're thinking about thinking), you'll concentrate some more, focus, more static, and then the station comes in, as clear as a bell.

You're not imagining it—you're not making it up, you're not straining at all to hear it—it's as simple, as obvious as holding a box or touching a rock. It's solid. It's real as real can be.

Those of you who already have experienced this kind of "knowing," whether through a voice, a sensation, or interpreting a symbol that comes into your life, are clear about its reality, and you also know that you can trust it and that it speaks truly.

We *all* have the ability to "know." *Every single one of us.*

How can you activate your internal antenna so you can receive messages from your intuitive voice?

We all experience this 'tuning in' differently. I am verbal—I live in the world of words. Language is my passion. I'm a writer.

But if you're a painter, you live in the world of color, imagery, themes. So if that's your intuitive way of connecting with the world, let the images come to you—don't seek words. Or if you're a musician, let the music of the spheres enter. We tend to think in language, but some of the most intuitive people I've met use other methods to "know"—including archetypes, nature, and art.

You'll need to find your own way.

My experience with my intuitive voice started when I was very young: I used to experience words or phrases randomly and fairly frequently. I did not know what they were; often the voices were so loud and clear, I'd turn around to see who had spoken. One time it was visual: I was on the school bus and abruptly I saw four letters in a lovely script forming before my eyes. First the L, then O, then V, then E. They hovered in front of me, glowing with the light of a very still sparkler. I even reached out to touch it, and it did not move, and I outlined the letters over and over, while they stayed there.

When I was a child, I called these phrases and images my "interruptions." I wrote them down, sensing something strange and interesting about them, but not having a clue as to what they were. I still remember some: when I was twelve it was "terracotta vase." When I was fourteen: "When will the blessingman stop?" Still others: "I thought you knew her *now*!" And: "Leave the door open!"

It wasn't until I was in my fifties that I began taking these messages seriously. I practiced opening the door to these voices. For me, my door was the tarot. Using tarot cards stimulates both the active focus of meditative thinking and the day-dreamy (letting the colors and symbols activate your unconscious). When I tune in to this completely, another voice entirely—not mine—speaks through me.

The first time it happened was after I'd listened to a lecture by Dennis Klocek called "Honoring the Dead." In it he talked about the twelve evolutionary sounds—the consonants that he says created our universe. (These are based on the Ancient Greek mathematician and mystic Pythagoras's insights about the universe being based on the number twelve—and on the twelve signs of the zodiac.) Dennis Klocek asked twelve people in the audience to form a circle and gave them each one of the sounds, beginning with the very first one: B. He then had them speak their sounds, randomly.

After that he asked seven more people to come up, and form a smaller circle inside the larger one. To this group he gave seven vowel sounds (these are associated with the seven planets). The consonants circled one way, the planets circled the other, and both formed their sounds out loud, randomly. Some got loud, some got soft—sometimes I heard meaning, or emphasis, and then every now and then a word or phrase.

After the lecture was over I inwardly re-listened to the evolutionary sounds that had created our universe. Smoothly, they formed into phrases, sentences, coherent poems, and lines of beauty inside me.

This is the essence of tuning in—it is effortless. It happens not when you're breathing in, but when you're breathing out. It happens not when you're chasing after it, but when you let it come to you.

The intuitive mind is a sacred gift and the rational mind is a faithful servant. Don't honor the servant and forget the gift. —attr. to Albert Einstein

Practice, Listen, Improvise

Practice: *Become familiar with archetypes*

Carl Jung describes our psyche as being divisible into three parts: The first is the ego, which relates to the world through our personal conscious minds. The second, our personal unconscious, includes anything which is not presently conscious, but actually could be made conscious, through hypnosis, therapy, dream analysis, or any other triggers to memory.

The third part that makes up our soul life is a human "collective unconscious." From ancient myths to our most recent literature, archetypes permeate the human soul in ways that we don't always understand. Our connection to these primordial archetypes influences how we respond to imagery—like color and number, for example—but we don't necessarily know why we instinctually respond that way.

But they are not biological instincts so much as a great universal human spirit that blankets the world in which we live and our soul's journey through it. Jung believed that all the most powerful ideas in history go back to archetypes, particularly those connected with religion and spirituality, but also those associated with science, philosophy, and ethics.

The archetypes that you need to begin to notice are innate, universal, and hereditary. They aren't things you need to "learn" but you *can* learn to recognize them, particularly through your emotional response to images. "It is the function of consciousness, not only to recognize and assimilate the external world through the gateway of the senses, but to translate into visible reality the world within us," Jung states in his book *The Structure of the Psyche*.

That is what you need to do now, at this stage of your journey. Recognize your emotional response to colors, numbers, patterns, fabric, stories. Children do this in a very intuitive way. Whereas a grown-up's first question to you at a party is probably going to be "What do you do?", a child's question is more likely "What is your favorite color?" And the response means something to that child.

Your inward response to a color triggers self-knowledge, and helps you to know how you can relate to the world around you in the most effective and happy way. An archetype is simply there, it's part of you—but when you bring it to the surface of your consciousness, you can use it to shape and create your inner life as you want it to be.

Jung identified four major archetypes, but also believed there was no limit to the number that may exist. I'm going to tread lightly through these basic four and then suggest some more, but what is most important is to realize that it is your personal experience of these archetypes that turns them into something substantive, inspiring, and real.

The Self

Very simply put, the self is an archetype that represents the unification of the unconsciousness and consciousness in you. The creation of the self occurs through integration of our many selves, or as Jung termed it, "*individuation.*"

It's also the unification between our selves and our spirit, which must also be integrated. Jung felt the symbols of a circle or square represented the self best. Children draw stick figures, and the symbol of a cross is used for a symbol of "life" in Ancient Egypt. You will need to discover your own symbol for the self.

The Shadow

The Shadow is particularly fascinating, because we tend to deny the shadows in ourselves and project them onto others. When we recognize our shadow not as bad or evil, but as mysterious, wild, untamed, fearful, dark, and scary—and try to integrate it within the more ideal conscious self—we become powerful indeed. That is an integration of self that brings a deep self-understanding and harmony.

Our shadow may appear in dreams as something or someone who is fearsome or despicable. Why is it really there? What is it really representing?

Don't just pay attention to your favorite color, but also to the one that makes you turn away in disgust. Honor that dislike. If something horrifies you, wonder why that is. Don't just take it for granted that it's horrifying to everyone. It's personal.

Your shadow, like a force of nature, is amoral—neither good nor bad. So don't judge your shadow: embrace it. When you encounter symbols of your shadow (snakes, demons, dragons, monsters guarding the entrance to a pool of water or a dark cave), stop and say hello.

Your shadow side is your friend—without it you would not be a human being. The worst thing you could do is repress it or project it onto someone else.

But treat it like a friend and you'll become whole.

The Anima and Animus

Jung believed that we all have both male and female qualities in us and that if we could integrate the two in ourselves we would feel wholly human. The anima and animus, as he termed them, represent the female and male qualities, respectively, in the collective unconscious of the world. In a man's unconscious, it finds expression as a female (*anima*) and in the unconscious of a woman it's masculine (*animus*).

Together, they are referred to as syzygy or divine couple, representing wholeness, unification, one-ness. The anima and animus is a way of describing your soul and is a way of communicating with the collective unconscious.

The Persona

The word persona comes from a Latin word meaning mask. We all wear masks when we set forth to greet the outer world. We have to or we'd be far too open and vulnerable. But we don't want to fall into the trap of believing the mask we put on is really ourselves.

We use a mask to impress, convince, engage, win.

It's crucial in this journey that you differentiate between your mask and your soul.

Other Archetypes

Archetypes shift, overlap, or alter, depending on where you are in the moment.

- A mother archetype might be symbolized by nature and fertility, the earth mother. She is nurturing, kind.
- A father archetype is an authority figure, perhaps stern and controlling.
- A child archetype represents something young, beginning, innocent. In the tarot, he is represented by the Fool—the being who innocently sets out on his great adventure without really knowing where he is going.

Many archetypes are story characters. For example, a hero represents your ego, and you'll find him out defending honor, rescuing maidens, or conquering the shadow of dragons and demons. A young maiden represents purity and innocence—also desire.

- There is also an animal archetype, representing humanity's relationships with the animal world. Aesop's Fables describe these archetypes best—highly recommended reading. You'll meet the faithful dog, the sly fox, the patient crow.

Here are a few archetypes of the tarot:

- The Magician: Magic and power. The trickster.
- The High Priestess: Intuition, the Anima, the unconscious female element of the male.
- The Lovers: Union of opposites. The Soul. Both the Anima and Animus.
- The Chariot: Hard work and victory. The Warrior.

- The Wheel of Fortune: Change, moving in circles. Fate and Destiny.
- Death: Change, transition. Rebirth
- The Tower: Chaos, unwanted change.

Listen: *Notice Things*

When I was growing up sometimes my mother would exclaim, "Look at that! Three crows!"

And I'd ask curiously, "What does it mean?"

Her response: "That's what you need to find out. What's important is that you notice everything. When you know, you'll know."

Noticing is essential for your process of discovering what you would do if there was nothing you had to do. Notice a color, a bird, a flower, a fragrance. Notice the dust on the windowsill. Go for the detail, without analyzing, without judging or trying to interpret it.

Noticing things activates a part of our souls that works in the great archetype of "symbol." Red is a symbol for passion or anger. The number two is a symbol for both separation (light and dark, for example) and for union.

But archetypes are much more wise and complex than a method of interpretation. Archetypes work on a deep level of your psyche. You don't have to "know" that red is the color of passion—you need to allow yourself to experience the vibration of the color and let it resonate in your soul. Gaze at a red rose: your inner experience is different than if you are looking at a black tulip.

If you see two birds on a branch you'll feel differently than if you see three or six or seven. See what happens when you notice the numbers in your life. Even numbers make you feel—even. Balanced. Harmonious. Perhaps stuck a little. Odd numbers push you on a bit because you want to get to that balance again. We need both.

Write down answers to the following questions:

What is your favorite color?

What is your favorite number?

What is your favorite animal?

What is your favorite tree or flower?

What is your favorite month?

Once we're grown-ups these questions seem frivolous. Silly. Unimportant. Worse, they seem selfish. Who cares what your favorite color is? Perhaps an interior decorator!

But *you* need to care. You need to recognize your own personal emotional response to things like colors and numbers because you'll become more harmonious in your self if you do. For example, when you see one bird on the branch of a tree, do you have a vague sense of loneliness and wonder "Where is its mate?" Or do you think of a star on stage, singing her hit song for the world to hear? Or is your feeling one of solitary peace and simplicity? Become conscious of your feelings when you're noticing what is going on around you.

Improvise: *Forget Everything You've Learned*

When I took my first surfing lesson in Hawai'i, my teacher showed me the technique while I was still on the beach. He made me practice the same steps, over and over, safe on the sand: how to lie on the board, how to paddle past the breaking waves, how to get to my knees when I was ready to catch a wave, then how to get to my feet, and how to balance.

At last he deemed me ready. He said, "Okay, you've learned all that. Now this is all you need to know: forget everything I just taught you. The waves and the board will do it for you."

He taught me the art of letting go.

After that, my experience of being out on the ocean on the crest of a wave was as freeing and exhilarating as flying.

Try it—if not with surfing, then with dancing.

We come back to the state of "effortless concentration" of Chapter 1.

Let go of everything you learned—and allow it to surface as intuition rather than interpretation.

That is the secret of knowing and of trusting that you know.

Consciousness succumbs all too easily to unconscious influences, and these are often truer and wiser than our conscious thinking. –C. G. Jung

3. Creating: *You are the artist of your life*

*The creative is the place where no one else has ever been. You have to leave the
city of your comfort and go into the wilderness of your intuition. What you'll
discover will be wonderful. What you'll discover is yourself.* —Alan Alda

B eing creative is essential to the journey. You aren't alive
unless you're artistic in some way, whether cooking a
delicious meal, having a sparkling conversation, shopping
creatively for a pair of shoes, painting, or writing a poem.

Being fully alive means being active with the many aspects of
yourself.

Everyone is creative in some way, whether it's in the kitchen or
in the garden, creative with numbers or with words. A teacher is
creative—so is a farmer, and so is a baby. We are all, in our heart
of hearts, artists.

Nature is the most profound door to your creativity, because
practically everything you experience in nature will resonate with
your intuition. Listen to a tree. Taste the wind. Imagine the
experience of an ant as it goes in and out of its hole.

On your journey to discovering what you would do if there was nothing you had to do, your creativity is at the heart of the matter. It's fundamental to the process of uncovering your heart's desire.

How can you do this?

To begin, experience color. (You could just as easily experience music, poetry, or fragrance, but I'm going to suggest you begin with the soul of color.)

In physics classes you learned about the mechanics of color, about its spectrum and wave lengths. But you don't need to know a lot about how color works in order for you to have a direct, immediate, and personal experience of color.

We experience contraction when we move from summer into winter, or from yellow into blue. We expand from winter into spring, from ice blue into April green; from the darkness of the longest night of the year to the joy of the longest day; from indigo blue into chrome yellow.

Yellow radiates out from any frame you try to put around it. It is light-hearted, joyous.

Blue moves inward.

Color tends to motion. You have to imagine color as being in motion because light itself is in motion. So is darkness. Watch a shadow.

Color is what happens when light and darkness meet. It flows from darker to lighter, and also in a circle, reflecting the time of day, the seasons or the year, and your own mood. Color appears in the activity that takes place between light and darkness. Our feeling life is a whole world of color in itself.

It feels blue when sad or glum; red in anger.

And so along the crescent of colors that is the rainbow, which rests right in the center of our world of color.

When colors move from light into darkness, they show up differently than when they pass from darkness into light. For instance, green grass tends to yellow in sunshine when the sun is behind it. When we gaze up into blue sky we're observing sheer sunlight in the atmosphere, light unopposed against the black backdrop of space.

But when we see red in the sky, it is because darkness has come between us and the yellow sun.

The circle of color we live in is reflected in part by the rainbow which we see as brightening to red, orange, yellow then darkening back to green, blue, indigo and on into the darkness of violet. The two ends of the rainbow merge in opposite ends of darkness. A human being, too, is such a meeting place. So is our little Earth.

Color is your rainbow slide into the warmth of the world. The light-filled colors of paint make connections between your inner radiance and the color-filled world of nature.

 Why do two colors, put one next to the other, sing? Can one really explain this? No. Just as one can never learn how to paint. —Pablo Picasso

Practice, Listen, and Improvise

Practice: *Paint with watercolors*

In this next practice I'm going to show you how to be creative using only water and color. Water-color paint is lovely and wet and therefore tends to motion. It can be kept clear and bright, reflecting your inner shine. You can experience yourself as a cloud of color.

For this practice you will need:

1. A large, white piece of watercolor paper
2. A half-inch size watercolor paint brush
3. 3 small jars (6 oz or so)
4. 1 larger jar of water

5. a small sponge
6. 3 tubes watercolor paints. You're only going to use primary colors. Begin with cobalt blue, crimson red, chrome yellow. (Later you can use cerulean blue, vermillion, and lemon yellow, for even hotter and colder contrasts.)

Getting ready:

Take the large piece of white watercolor paper. With a sponge , wet the paper well on both sides.

Press the paper onto the table.

Take your sponge and brush it across the paper so that it sticks to the table without wrinkles. Do this slowly and carefully, leaving no puddles. Don't rub too hard or you will break the surface.

Next take one of the small jars and squeeze a small dollop of yellow paint into it.

Add enough water to dilute the color, but allow it to remain strong and clear.

With sponge and brush by your side, you are set to begin.

Begin to paint:

Take your dry brush and gently waft it over the backs of both your hands. Do this lightly, with attention. This reminds you that the brush is not a wall-painter's tool, rather it is more like a magic wand.

Dip your brush neatly into your small jar of glowing color. Press the brush against the inside of the jar to squeeze off excess water.

Pick up your brush attentively. Painting is a way of getting you right into your physical body, and not just your eyes and head. Next, run your brush over your paper. Remember the softness of the brush on the back of your hands and imagine that the paper is experiencing that same softness.

The first time you paint, use only one color: yellow. Yellow has a laughing, cheerful disposition, tending always to formlessness. You start, in a sense, where you were as a child, before more complicated, darker colors permeated your soul.

Paint as many as four or five—or ten or twelve! paintings using only clear, strong yellow. You will find each time new discoveries and marvels from this one radiant source.

Start sometimes at the outside of your paper and work in. Then on another sheet, on another day, start with a round shape in the middle and radiate out. Watch the subtle changes of color as the yellow proceeds inwards or outwards. Enjoy the extra shine of the white paper. Deepen the yellow at the center, lighten it at the edges. Then try it the other way around. Is there a difference? Try to get the yellow in motion in this way.

Think of the sun, or a dandelion, or a yellow slicker in the rain. Attach yourself to the rich world of yellow. Do not feel you need to know more than this to start. The important thing is to be willing to start at the very beginning, to be willing to concentrate on one color at a time for a while, and to go through the basic experience that color offers by itself as completely as possible.

Color is experienced in two ways: the outer color on the paper, and the complementary color that emerges inwardly. As you brush yellow onto the paper, you inwardly produce the yellow's complementary color: violet.

How magical and mysterious and creative and yet *real* is that?

Fill the entire sheet of paper with yellow paint, leaving no white patches. You may think this interferes with your picture making, with your freedom as an artist, but filling the paper with color activates your will forces, giving you a feeling of physical control over the wonders of the world. It shows you that you know how to finish something you have begun. It introduces a sense of accomplishment. You will get into the habit of completing an activity—an innate human need that became distorted by interference from busy grown-ups and society and school bells from an early age.

This is the raw experience of color. You might think you'd produce better pictures if you took a big paint-box and used a variety of ready-made colors. But by doing it this way, you are experiencing something that existed before mixtures and before pictures.

This way of painting will make you feel more confident and self-reliant. You aren't painting what someone else is telling you to paint, you are making personal discoveries. *You* are the real creator.

After three or four sessions of yellow, start a new session using only the color blue. Ideally, think deeply about blue and different objects and feelings that are blue. Notice blueness in nature and in your home and in someone's eyes.

When everything is ready, proceed in the usual way. Wet the paper, mix blue paint with water, fill a large jar with clear water. Then start to paint blue in the center, lightly at first, but getting darker towards the edges, varying intensities.

Feel the beauty of blue. Do not forget the inner painting you are making within yourself at the same time. A blue world on paper stimulates a translucent orange inside you—a soft, vibrant, ethereal orange resonating in the core of your belly.

Starting with a circular form in the middle, gently bring the color further and further out. Next time, start from the outside and bring the color in. See how it looks and feels with a lighter blue in the central area. Watch the difference when the center is a darker blue.

As I said before, be sure to fill the paper entirely, so there are no white patches. Besides training the will to bring activities to completion, this creates a harmonious whole which will be reflected in the complementary painting which is being created deep within you. Completion of an activity helps to bring your moods within your own control.

After a few sessions of blue, introduce red. Enter into the mood of red. A sunset. Autumn leaves. Apples. Fire-engines. A favorite pillow. A new dress.

Then follow the same procedure as with yellow and blue.

Each shade of red finds its own complementary color within a wide range of greens: all the way from turquoise to emerald. Experience your inner green in all its richness.

Now it's time to move on to two colors:

Put a shape of yellow on one side of the paper. Clean your brush well in the water jar, and dip it into the blue. Paint a shape of blue on the opposite side, far apart. Don't let them touch. Sit back and contemplate the beauty of thse two colors. Watch them interact, not physically yet, but across the white expanse of paper.

Remember at this moment that the complementary colors are being subconsciously activated in you. Behind the picture being painted in front of your eyes, you are painting a second picture behind your eyes. It consists of your own special orange, that is the complementary of the blue on the paper, and your very own purple, the complementary of the yellow. These inner colors are of the quality of light, not pigment. They are transparent, and in motion.

Allow enough time for your inner experience of color to take place at a slow, deliberate pace. This not only gives your outer world more stability, but gives your inner one a chance to unfold.

Once again, slowly let your hand take up your paintbrush. With gentleness and concentration, bring the two colors closer together, first one, then the other, keeping the colors completely clean. Back and forth, back and forth, until they are just about to meet and run together.

When the colors finally run together, you will have created green!

Now *that* is creative.

At first, try to keep the two colors separate: clean and clear. This is not as easy as it sounds. Blue is hard to clean off the brush and your jar of water will be green before you know it. Notice it. When you paint with primary colors and try to keep green in its place, you understand why the world is so green. You are not the only one who has trouble keeping sunny yellow from mixing all the time with blue: nature has the same problem.

Once you've painted with blue and yellow and made green several times, and you are feeling the joy and confidence that a child might feel, try the same exercise using red and yellow. Take several sessions to get the full impact of this next experiment. This time you will discover and create the color orange.

Keep in mind that you have been experiencing orange colors of the utmost subtlety, inwardly, when you painted blue. Now you find it confirmed in the outer world, and realize that it is you who have made it actually appear.

This act affirms what poets and artists know, but which most of us forget, that *the truth of inner experience can be brought to the outer world and can be made to work peacefully and constructively with it.*

After blue and yellow, and red and yellow, give yourself a lovely long time with red and blue, creating purple on the page.

And then proceed to use all three primary colors at once.

There is such a variety of ways of using these three colors so relate to them in your own way for a time. Create your very own connections with each color, singly, in pairs and in threes.

On occasion, but gently, not critically, remind yourself to keep brushes clean, to keep colors on the paper from getting muddy by too much mixing and brushing. Keep imagining your inner canvas and be sure these have a chance to remain whole, clear and colorful.

When painting, proceed slowly. The entire process might take twenty to thirty minutes, while only part of those might be taken up in actually painting the picture.

Take delight in preparation and cleaning up. It should be a fun part of the main activity of putting paintbrush to paper. If you realize that in order to paint you have to get your materials prepared and later carefully cleaned and stored, you'll find yourself experiencing pleasure in all three aspects of being creative—the preparation and the putting away, as well as the actual painting.

If you tend to paint quickly, slow down. If you're going very slowly, speed up a bit. Learn balance. If you're shy, you may find your colors tentative. Make them stronger. If you're exhuberant and your colors are powerful, mix them more translucently.

Everything you do is beautiful. You are the same as your painting. Don't objectify it, as an artist might, discriminating and criticising as you go along. The finished results rarely tell you all there is to say about the pleasures and satisfactions encountered in the creating of a painting. It is the experience of the color that matters—it is not the finished product for which you are striving.

For this practice, only use your three primary colors: yellow, blue and red. To use more than these three is to dilute your experience of the basic moods and feelings in the world of color and also removes the thrill of discovery.

The world of color is rich and vast. Allow yourself to experience as much of the three primary colors as possible.

Pure experience is hard to come by today. It tends to be pre-packaged. Here in your painting hour, pure discovery can be reached once again.

Verbal explanations tend to take some of the fun away from activities like this. It is like being told what a birthday present is before you have a chance to unwrap it. Very briefly, though, I'll tell you that the watercolor activities that I've outlined above are based mainly on Goethe's *Theory of Color* that the spiritual scientist Rudolf Steiner integrated into Waldorf Education. If you attended a Waldorf school as a child, as I did, this kind of therapeutic watercolor painting was a standard part of the curriculum. This section of my book is drawn in great part from a book that my mother, Jane Winslow Eliot, wrote for teachers on how to teach painting to young children.

Other artists who were influenced by Goethe's work include the wonderful British painter J. M. W. Turner (who extensively annotated Goethe's theory) and the Russian abstractionist Vassily Kandinsky who carried these color impulses forward into modern art. But all this additional information is for you to find out about later, if and when you want to. The experience itself is the point here; let theories come in on a later train.

Listen: *Write in your journal*

I can't stress enough the importance of journaling. As you undergo this journey, you need to be actively connecting with the process in some way. Writing down the activities, and your responses to them, creates a mirror that reflects what happens in an objective, loving way. You begin to regard yourself more as the child you once were, and to be as affectionate toward your effort—clumsy and difficult as it might appear at first—to find your heart's desire.

Be creative in your journaling. If you've been using one color to write with, try another. Write in circles on the page. Skip a page. Glue a leaf or a ribbon onto the page. Journal by doodling or just write down a list of verbs instead of making up sentences.

Improvise: *Being creative is a way to be free*

The remarkable thing about creativity is that the process is actually one of freedom. Your canvas is blank—ready and waiting. Whether it's your piece of paper, or a guitar or piano, or your garden that awaits, you are always free to create.

Your task now is to improvise, using the soul of color, in other creative realms that you haven't explored before or that you want to experience more deeply.

Begin with what you love doing most in the whole world. For me it's writing novels. Getting lost in a story, bringing characters to life, spending long days in another world as I create cities and countries and imagine relationships and events—for me, there's no greater feeling of satisfaction.

In order to create one has to live fully in the here and now. One has to feel passionately, to observe, and learn, and sometimes to know things that perhaps you'd rather not, to throw one's heart into life.

This is not only true of writing: it's true of cooking. If you want to create a great meal, the absorption in the ingredients, the mixing, the tasting, the serving, and the eating is an orchestra of wonder and passion.

Try something new. Involve yourself completely.

Being creative sets you free.

The world is but a canvas to the imagination. —Henry David Thoreau

The most common way people give up their power is by thinking they don't have any. –Alice Walker

4. Empowering: *Who's in charge?*

There is another aspect of your human nature that you need to develop after you've imbued yourself with "creativity" and that is "power."

In order to experience the realities of living in the tangible world of responsibility and control, and living within a society that tends to be hierarchical and community-minded, you'll need to find your place in it.

Power is the most misunderstood quality of being human. You might imagine power as corrupting, cruel. You might conjure up images of Roman emperors, or generals, or your particular someone who's in a position of authority.

Or power may be something you wish you had more of.

But personal power is different. Personal power means you have the courage, strength, and the ability to create the life you want.

Most of us feel as though our lives are out of our control. We long for a larger income, or to meet an ideal mate, to be healthy and prosperous, to have the domicile of our dreams.

But for most of us the grass is always greener.

Think about it. If you could live anywhere, where would you live? What is your dream house? A castle or a farmhouse in Vermont? A villa? If you really think it through, do you want to leave your friends, your community and move to an island in Greece? Often we glamorize what might be fun for a vacation, but not more than that. You do have the power to move; you choose not to for various reasons that are just as important to you.

You have a lot more power than you realize. Your power is infinite. Even if you're caretaking an invalid or you're in what seems like a dead-end job or you're stuck in a loveless marriage, you are freer than you realize.

What it takes is a different mindset. A powerful mindset.

If you could do anything, what would you do?

Imagine the possibilities.

I love power. But it is as an artist that I love it. I love it as a musician loves his violin, to draw out its sounds and chords and harmonies.

–Napoleon Bonaparte, as characterized in
Havelock Ellis's *The Dance of Life*

Practice, Listen, and Improvise

Practice: *Empower yourself*

Write answers to the following two questions with complete freedom. No one has to read these except you.

The most important aspect is stretching your imagination to picture yourself as a free individual in control of your life, even if you think—right now—that this is impossible.

These two questions have to do with the fundamental qualities that most of us want power over. I know this because during my many years as a psychic consultant, these are the questions that are asked repeatedly, by the richest, the poorest, the most famous, the most humble people in the world. It doesn't matter who or what or where you are, these are the questions that matter most.

Love/relationships

Choose three relationships that *right now* are the most important in your life. Make two lists, and in one list write all the things that you find distressing or frustrating about the relationship. Remember to do this from your vantage point. In other words, don't write "He's a mean person," but "I feel he's mean to me." By placing people and relationships into the context of your own feelings, you'll have an easier time sorting out the relationship's effect on you, and what you can do about it, rather than feeling yourself to be a victim of unalterable circumstances. Delve into all the details of the *why* you feel he's mean. Give examples.

Then write a list of all the things that are positive about this same person or relationship. Again, go into details and include examples. Take your time. This might not happen in just one sitting.

Sometimes our emotions confuse the reality of a situation. By bringing those emotions into the light of consciousness, and hanging them out to dry, so to speak, you may be surprised by what you find. Issues that were hidden away in a cupboard of anxiety, dislike, confusion, or misery begin to fade or shrink. Affection and harmony may become stronger.

If that's not the case, you may see a relationship more clearly and realize that it may not be a healthy one. A choice may have to be made—but you don't have to make it yet. You just need to realize that a choice may have to be made about who you really want in your life, and that you have the *power* to choose.

Work/career

Now do the same exercise around your work situation. If you're retired or a trust-fund baby and you don't have to "go to work," you'll still find some aspect of your life that involves work. Do you have a spouse who needs care? Do you manage a family or a house? Are you a volunteer at the local library?

Focus on this work and write a list of all the things you dislike about your daily work or that you find most challenging. Now write a list of all the things you love about it.

Listen: *Analyze the situation*

Compare your lists. Sometimes an aspect will be on both lists. For example: "I have to leave the house every morning" might be something good—and yet on some occasions it might be something you really would prefer not to have to do.

Now write a brief paragraph of your immediate visceral response to these two lists. If the negatives far outweigh the positives, you might write something like: *I have got to get the hell out of here.*

Don't self-edit as you write your emotional response. Let your intuitive voice surface. You might be surprised, though, at how much positive energy emerges and makes you realize that there are a lot of aspects of your work that you enjoy, that sustain and nourish you, and that you are delighted to be involved in.

If you write down "I am irritated by how Lulu criticizes my outfit all the time," you may find that the irritation shrinks into insignificance as you stare at the words on the page. Or they may loom larger and you may come to understand that the activity of the person is insignificant, but that they are a drain on your psyche and you do not want to waste your energy in being with them any longer.

What can you do if you are stuck with a boss who belittles you or if you're living with a housemate who is disparaging or discouraging?

This is what you'll realize as you empower yourself more and more: You don't have to be stuck with anyone or anything that belittles or hurts you. I don't mean you necessarily have to quit or move out. I mean that *you* can change. You can feel powerful and in charge. You'll be amazed at how by turning your imagination inside out, you can change other peoples' feelings about you, and actions toward you.

Improvise: *Keep going*

In addition to relationships and work, the other areas most of us want power over are our physical health, financial security, and spiritual path. You can create similar lists for any area of your life that is making you feel disconnected or powerless.

As you do this, focus on your own dynamic energy, your ambition, your markers of success, your worldly achievements in a way that empowers you. Instead of feeling at the mercy of society, family, structures, or childhood expectations, turn yourself inside out and imagine *yourself* as the source of all these important aspects of your life, and everything around you serving your actions, achievements, and goals.

I knew a woman who felt intimidated by a colleague—even though she owned her own business and could fire any employee at any time. In visiting her office I saw at once how it was her own perception of being stuck that was preventing a feeling of pleasure and accomplishment. I suggested she hire a Feng Shui consultant to find ways to change her office space. Something so simple and practical shifted her way of seeing her work and all her colleagues. She felt empowered enough to fire someone who brought the rest of her employees down, to promote another, and to sort out what had become a rut of misery in her daily world. You are at work for a third of your life. Enjoy it—even if it's by bringing a vase of flowers in or hanging up a painting that you love.

Ultimately, the secret to personal power rests in your ability to experience happiness.

All work is meaningless without a feeling of joyful satisfaction. Not a giddy high, but a sense of self-worth, compassion for others, and clear conscience. That is real power.

And no matter how much you love someone, if they belittle or denigrate you, that's not going to make you feel powerful.

Your personal power comes from experiencing joy.

So, be with people who make you feel good about yourself, who acknowledge your worth, your beauty, your kindness, your creativity, your intuition, and your courage. Surround yourself with colleagues who admire, respect, challenge, and reward you. Feel good about your office and surrounding: you deserve to create it in a way that reflects the powerful, strong, active human being that you are.

Choose people and work that are empowering—and you'll *be* empowered.

Our deepest fear is not that we are inadequate. Our deepest fear is that we are powerful beyond measure. It is our light, not our darkness that most frightens us. We ask ourselves, 'who am I to be brilliant, gorgeous, talented, and fabulous?' Actually, who are not to be? ...As we let our own light shine, we unconsciously give other people permission to do the same. As we are liberated from our own fears, our presence automatically liberates others.
—Marianne Williamson

We are what we repeatedly do. Excellence, then, is not an act, but a habit.
—Aristotle

5. Committing: *The initiation of the daily life*

If you're reading this book, it is more likely that you want to break with tradition, not create it. So it may seem odd that rhythms and rituals are part of the process of discovering what you ultimately want to be doing, thinking, and feeling in your life.

Rhythms, however, when used wisely, can be inwardly freeing.

We live in rhythm. We live in cyclical rhythms, daily, even hourly rhythms, lunar and seasonal rhythms. Our brains are programmed so that an hour and a half marks the limit of our ability to fully concentrate. This is a good thing to know because if a meeting goes on past that length, you're pretty much wasting everyone's time. End it. Take a break—and regroup later. That's a simple rhythm to be aware of.

The same with our inner clock—don't schedule an energetic or important meeting at 2 p.m. (or 2 a.m. for that matter) if you can help it. Your energy is at its lowest at that time, and the best thing you can do then is take a siesta or relax with a book or light conversation.

Because you're human, you are free to create your own rhythms and not be solely at the mercy of Nature. This is something Susan West Kurz writes about in her book *Awakening Beauty*. Beauty, she says, is not about creams and cosmetics, but about incorporating rhythms into your daily life. Give your body rhythmic rest that allows your natural enzymes and hormones to act and react with each other. Create a ritual using lavender by putting a few drops on a wet washcloth and breathing it in before you go to bed. You'll find you sleep better.

After a while, your brain responds automatically to the fragrance of lavender and you'll be ready for sleep even if you are stressed.

If you're rested and calm, you feel more alive and beautiful—and that is reflected in your face.

Your task is to find what rhythm or ritual gives you the space and the freedom to do what you love. If you don't honor the simple things you enjoy, they tend to disappear, and then sometimes reappear as anger or sadness or irritation.

Find space for the things you enjoy. It may be bathing, for example. You might choose to create a ritual around that, rather than hopping in and out of the shower because it wakes you up in the morning or because you feel you "have to" hurry.

Or you may love to read. Create a space for that—not last thing at night before you go to sleep when you're too tired to stay awake, but at a time that you can truly enjoy the experience of reading.

Do you love to garden? Even that is often a "have to" chore. "I have to mow." "I have to weed." Create a rhythm so that at a certain time of day it's your rhythmic task and you begin to anticipate and see it as a time to enjoy.

By creating small, meaningful rhythms and rituals in your day, week, month, and year, you find more meaning in your life. You are blowing away the cobwebs of have-tos, shoulds, and stresses, and instead allowing joy and significance to take their place.

The initiation of the daily life.

Initiation rites are different today than they were in olden times, when you might be left in the heart of a pyramid for three days or you were trained from the age of six to keep the lamp oil burning. Nowadays you are being asked to live a daily life that is full and rich and busy and exhausting. How can you turn that into a rite of initiation?

My mother used to call it the initiation of the daily life. You do it by bringing your consciousness to the details and the experiences that happen throughout the course of your day. Notice things—pay attention. When you notice things, you're opening yourself up to a magical experience of co-creating your experience. Everything matters—and what doesn't matter can fall by the wayside.

Here's an example: Like many couples, my husband and I have spent many hours arguing about whether it is more environmentally responsible to wash dishes using the dishwasher or to wash them by hand. Everyone we spoke to about this had an opinion—whether it was the amount of water we used or the detergent or the electricity. This we learned for a fact: there's no definitive answer as to the efficacy of either method.

However, in the course of my research I discovered that the Dalai Lama had been asked the same question. His response? *What is important is that you ask yourself why you are washing the dishes.*

In other words, *paying attention is what matters.* Loving the process of cleanliness and the sparkle of sunshine on soapsuds or enjoying the hum of the dishwasher—it doesn't matter which you choose as long as you do it with attention, care, respect, and ritual. In other words, don't throw your dishes into the dishwasher, wishing they'd just go away. Don't waste water in the sink. Water is precious. Sing, chat, make it a ritual, especially with children! If dishes are washed with thoughtful, loving care, you'll find that your children will always love that particular task.

Love your duty. Love your work. Love the daily things that have to get done.

> *We are beings of rhythm, and rhythm supports and carries life... You will begin to find that you become more creative, as well as more efficient with your time, once you have a structure for the week.* —Susan West Kurz

Practice, Listen, and Improvise

Practice: *Create a ritual*

Choose one thing that you don't particularly enjoying doing, but that you have to do almost every day. This could be commuting to work, cleaning—whatever. If there's nothing that comes to mind, choose something you are indifferent to.

Look at that activity from a different perspective. Think about the positive aspects of it. If you're commuting in heavy traffic, how about listening to an audio book or enjoying the opportunity to daydream?

What is interesting about this process of discovering what you would do if there was nothing you had to do, is that it is not as though you have to turn your whole life around, or move to a distant land, or quit a job you don't like. What you need to do is let your life fall into place around you, like the petals in a kaleidoscope.

Now notice a single simple task or quality that you love. This might be something you often dismiss—like the smell of soap or glancing at an affirmation you've taped onto your mirror.

Notice. Be attentive.

When you feel ready, create a ritual around something that you really *do* want to commit to. It may be as small as singing a song at least once a day or five minutes of yoga every morning, or saying "I love you" to yourself in the mirror.

Several years ago I committed to Writing as the thing I realized I wanted to do if there was nothing I had to do. Looking back, it amazes me that this was even a question for me. When wasn't I writing? But the writing itself had ups and downs, not just because I had to squeeze it into what was a much-too-busy life, but also because of my uncertainty about what I wanted to write—what would get published—who would edit—and so forth.

I actually created a wedding ceremony for my marriage to Mr. Write. I purchased a ring to remind me of my vow, and I spoke the words out loud. I committed to cherishing and loving writing for the rest of my life. I committed to writing "in sickness and health," meaning that even if I was blocked or anxious or "too busy," I would still write. Since that day I have written three things every morning: my dream journal, a poem or fiction piece—sometimes short, sometimes long, and daily happinesses (these are brief, evocative imaginations of a magical or natural sort, that keep my way of seeing and experiencing the world supple and fresh and that I post on my website and share with friends and strangers.)

No matter where I am or how tired or busy I am, I am committed to this writing ritual, and it has become as essential as brushing my teeth or taking a walk.

Listen: *Words matter*

Your ritual doesn't have to be a marriage ceremony, but it needs to be meaningful. You can do it with others around you or alone. You can be the messenger from the divine, the witness, and the officiator. What matters is that it's made *real*.

Your ritual is made concrete through the use of language. Words are things, stated Maya Angelou, and she is right. Words not only are symbols representing something real, they *are* real. They create reality.

Here's why. Until words have declared something to be that something, it isn't. Take marriage, for example. Until two people are 'pronounced' husband and wife, they aren't.

A knight could not be a knight until he had been dubbed a knight by the king. And if you were a king, but you did not know it and nor did anyone else, you would not be a king.

Words create things.

This is why the ritual you create for the daily activity that you commit to has to be written down, signed, sealed, and saved.

Every now and again, take it out again, and remind yourself of your vow.

Improvise: *Slow down*

Slow down. By slowing down, you'll actually create more time for yourself.

You may say you don't have time to do this. Your day is full, and adding a ritual or paying attention to a detail is time consuming. So I'll tell you something about time. *You can create it.*

You can create as much of it as you want.

Our idea that we have to 'rush' is completely in our heads. We are always in charge of our own time.

Here are the three practices that will help you acquire control and give you the magical ability to create as much time as you want or need to do anything you want or need to.

The first practice is simple. First thing in the morning, make your beverage of choice, have a seat, and gaze into the cup or mug with a lover's eyes. Really look at it. (If it's in a plastic container or travel cup, take the lid off.) Smell the fragrance. Touch the tip of your tongue to its enticing warmth.

Now, take a spoon (even if you don't use sugar), and circle the spoon five times in one direction, then five times in the other.

When you're done, drink your beverage.

You've just created a ritual that has *added* time to your day, not subtracted it.

It may seem paradoxical, but by taking more time, you make more time. If you're panting to keep up, then you're always going to feel stressed and pressed for time. If you slow down, give yourself more time to get from hither to thither, if you stop rushing through your activities, the amount of time you have to do things will increase exponentially.

More magic!

Les Mots

Where do words come from?
From what scraping friction were they born?
What match lit their fuse?
What winds drove them into our mouths?

Sometimes
they cling to each other, screaming
they swell in lamentations
they become mist on the windows of dead houses
they become crystallized nuggets of sorrow on dead lips
they attach to a fallen star
they carve out a hole in nothingness
they breathe in the souls of those led astray

The words are rocky tears
keys of the first doors
grumbling in caves
lending their uproar to tempests
and their silence to bread baked alive.

Vénus Khoury-Ghata
(tr. Samantha Stier)

Here is the Divine Dichotomy...
The way to 'get there' is to 'be there'.
Just be where you choose to get!'
It's that simple. –Neale Donald Walsch

6. Choosing: *Be guided by your inner compass*

I magine you are an empty vessel, and that you can choose to put in that vessel only that which is sweet and meaningful.

Would you put a museum in the vessel?

Or a nap?

Or a concert?

An adventure?

What is your passion?

How do you choose what to do?

Become conscious of how you make decisions.

Let's start with something simple. Cleaning the kitchen, for example. Everyone has a different method, timing, and certainly different 'feelings' about this important task. Previous generations never dreamed of going to bed with a dirty kitchen. Not all that long ago, refrigerators did not exist, so extra food had to be sealed from animals and stored somewhere cool. It simply wasn't safe to have a dirty kitchen. Keeping a clean kitchen was an essential part of community, family, and home.

Now it's more personal. We have other things to do. If a friendly neighbor drops by, but there's a stack of dirty dishes on the kitchen counter, do you stop to talk to your friend or do you turn him away so you can finish your chore?

If your young child has homework to do and at the same time is exhausted and needs to sleep, what would you advise her to do?

If you are choosing between watching a television show and taking a walk in the woods on a late summer evening, what would you do?

How do you decide?

A surprising amount of mental chatter tends to drown out your inner guide, and your inner guide is trying to let you know what you would find the most satisfying way to go.

More often than not, your inner compass does not communicate with you verbally. It's more like a gut feeling. Your verbal brain processes around 40 bits of data per second, but your nonverbal part of our brain processes 10 million bits of data per second. This is why you can "sense" danger or you "just know" something. Your inner compass is communicating with you nonverbally, which means it's faster, more alert, more trustworthy.

So trust it.

My husband was passionate about old vinyl records and when we lived in New York City back in the eighties we spent many days walking the streets while he hunted records and I hunted old books. He used to be able to 'smell' a record from several blocks away. I called it "smelling" because I was continually amazed at his ability to zero in on a box of records in the back of a funky store and pull out a find. His intuition—and his trust in that intuition—continues to astound me to this day.

I used to tease him about his sense of smell, likening him to a hound dog, but now I know that he was trusting an inner compass, that his passion for records guided him.

When your feelings or instincts are in direct opposition to what your mind is telling you through words, what do you choose?

Your inner compass is guiding you through your "unihipili"—your subconscious, intuitive part of yourself. Pay attention when you feel a sinking sensation in your stomach, or a sudden tiredness, or a vague regret. If you continue to ignore the directional signals, eventually the mental chatter that's instructing you to go the wrong way will only be silenced by you becoming sick, anxious, or depressed. But if you follow the way your intuition tells you, you'll feel confident and optimistic.

Trust your compass. It will show you the way you need to go, and it's not hard to learn how to use it.

> *There is a voice inside of you*
> *That whispers all day long,*
> *"I feel this is right for me,*
> *I know that this is wrong."*
> *No teacher, preacher, parent, friend*
> *Or wise man can decide*
> *What's right for you-just listen to*
> *The voice that speaks inside."*
>
> —Shel Silverstein

Practice, Listen, and Improvise

Practice: *Using your compass*

Here are three keys to practicing using your inner compass:

Know the difference: There are two ways of knowing—the knowledge that comes from outside yourself and the knowledge that comes from within. You need to be able to recognize the difference between them. The first is based on your mental state: how much you respect someone's advice, perhaps, or something you have studied for many years. But your inner compass rests in calm. It makes sense. It feels good and wise. It makes you feel calm. Exhilarated. Present. Sometimes it may also feel as though you are in some sort of slow motion. When my mother was dying in the hospital, I wanted to bring her home to die. There was nothing else that could be done. And yet, my home was 3,000 miles away, there was no place for her to go, there were many obstacles, yet I was utterly calm and certain: she *had* to die at home. And we worked it out so that she did.

Be in the present: sometimes all it takes to recognize the voice of your inner guide is to put aside your fear of the future or regret about the past and focus entirely on the present moment. When you're conducting a symphony, nothing else enters your head but the music and the orchestra. When you're about to shoot a ball into a basket, that's all that there is. If you need a refresher on *being here now*, take out your juggling balls again!

Practice. Practice using your inner compass on a daily basis. Listen to your body signals of distress—honor a headache or a vague feeling of unease. Don't always think it's your fault if something doesn't feel right. Practice using your instinct. Become aware of smells and sounds—anything may trigger your inner compass and gently urge you in a new direction. The more you practice trusting your intuition, the stronger it will appear to you.

Listen: *You are your own best guide*

Imagine you're lost in the desert and you have with you only a compass and an acquaintance who chatters nonstop. The compass tells you that north—where you're headed—is the way to go. Your friend urges you to take a road that looks easier to navigate with your camel. You know it's the wrong way, but the noise of your friend's chatter is hard to tune out.

This is because

- the chatter makes logical sense
- your friend seems reasonable
- you feel doubtful about not knowing the right way *for sure*
- you are ingrained to obey the word "should"
- you don't want to hurt someone's feelings

As you arrive at a moment in which you have to make a decision, pause and take out this list. Cross off any of the choices you have available to you that seem prompted by these voices.

Then see what you have left.

Which choice comes from a gut feeling, or an instinct, or a natural inner sense of relief or satisfaction?

Learn to trust it. Test it out—maybe you won't always be right. Does that matter? Not as much as the practice of learning to trust your inner guide.

Improvise: *When you're stuck, use a pendulum*

Using a pendulum was a breakthrough for me when I was first learning to trust my inner compass. I was in the throes of depression, I had two young children, was struggling financially, and my husband left me very free to make my own decisions—which was not what I thought I wanted back then. Often, I found myself paralyzed with indecision. Should I take the children to Washington Square Park or should we stay home?

Should I buy broccoli or spinach? Should I call my mother or not?

When you are suffering from a lack of confidence, having to choose can be extremely debilitating.

When a strange man showed up in my life and—seemingly out of the blue—showed me how to use a pendulum, I was skeptical. I did not believe that divine intervention or the universe or any higher being could possibly be interested in whether or not I bought broccoli for dinner.

But I used it anyway because *it made my choice for me.*

Using the pendulum provided me with a doorway into serenity in the realm of decision-making. I realized it did not matter to anyone else whether I bought broccoli or spinach. But what did *I* feel like cooking and tasting?

I realized these decisions come from me, not a "should" or what my kids would like, or a longing for my husband to advise me. Our task is to honor our own desires and longings.

Let your desire inspire you.

What is yours?

We humans continuously confront defining moments in our lives. At these
moments it's important to make the right choices. When we do, we're able to
manifest miracles and produce transformation in ourselves and others.
–Azim Noordin Khamisa

A ship in harbor is safe, but that is not what ships are built for.
                                                        –John A. Shedd

7. Traveling: *Going on an adventure*

You're on your way.

You've surrounded yourself with people who give you the nurturing, encouraging support you need, and you fill your days and nights with activities that you care about. You've begun to know what matters to you.

You've begun to trust your old-fashioned compass—your *inner* compass—to carry you in the direction that leads to your authenticity and happiness.

Now do something different. Go somewhere new, somewhere you've never been.

Explore a new experience, without judgment, without assessing whether it's good or bad or whether it makes sense. Just be adventurous for a while.

Our brains are programmed to receive verbal messages of obedience from the time we were born. *Be careful! Watch out! Don't say that! How dare you! Behave!*

Rarely are our brains charged with instructions like *"Go for it!" "Take a risk!" "Be yourself!" "Be authentic!" "Trust yourself!" "Listen to your Inner Voice!" "You know what's right!" "Be brave!"*

Try it. Step out on a limb. Try a new experience just for the adventure. If travel to another town or country is not feasible, travel through reading about a place that is new to you. Find a new place to hike, a new restaurant, and make a new friend.

As you explore this entirely new situation, be conscious of your inner voice. Not the scared, uh-oh voice, but the voice that says, "Go this way!" or "Try that one!"

> *Your time is limited, so don't waste it living someone else's life. Don't be trapped by dogma which is living with the results of other peoples' thinking. Don't let the noise of others' opinions drown out your own inner voice. And, most importantly, have the courage to follow your heart and intuition. They somehow already know what you truly want to become. Everything else is secondary.* —Steve Jobs

Practice, Listen, and Improvise

Practice: *Be an explorer*

No matter how silly or farfetched or seemingly inappropriate your longing is, you need to acknowledge it. This may take some time, because often our deepest longings and desires are hidden under layers of what we know we ought to desire. It's time to dig them out.

First, make a list of five places you'd like to visit. Paris? Vermont? Tahiti? Write a few words about why you'd like to go there. It's possible that after looking at your list you will realize that there may be other ways to experience what you want to get out of your trip. For example, say you want to go to Vermont to visit a favorite cousin. Perhaps you don't have to travel all that way after all: you can call her instead, or invite her to visit you.

Be honest with yourself. Don't imagine that Paris is a vague destination that everyone would enjoy. Be personal about how you imagine a trip there. Get a guide book, and go through all the things you'd like to do and the atmosphere you imagine experiencing while you're there. Cocktails on the Champs Elysée? Walking along the Seine?

Perhaps as you write your reasons for choosing Paris as a destination you realize that you want to go to Paris because you love French cuisine. Your culinary longing might be satisfied by going to a delightful French restaurant or buying a cookbook and experimenting with some recipes.

Second, make a list of five activities you enjoy doing more than anything in the world. This might be 'do nothing' or 'build a house.' Again, write a few words about why you want to do these activities.

If you love to work in your garden, ask yourself why that is. Do you love to get your hands covered with dirt as you dig for carrots or potatoes? Do you love the brown earth, the sun on your back, the smell of wild strawberries wafting past your nose, the sound of the nearby brook?

You may choose to do nothing simply because you're exhausted—not because you really enjoy doing nothing. Or maybe not. Get to the heart of the matter.

Third, make a list of five people you enjoy being with more than anyone else in the world. This one is tricky, because most people will write down their lover or their child before anyone else. But once you've written down the names of the people you love most in the world, pause, and do the exercise again. Those of us who have children may all agree that raising children is the best experience of our lives, but there are times when being a parent is terrifying, grueling, and exhausting. If you could be with *anyone* for a few hours on a desert island, would it be with your child, over whom you'd be worrying and fussing? Or with your spouse, who might be yelling at you for getting him or her into this fix?

Maybe if you could be with anyone in the world it would be with a childhood friend or a great-grandmother or a favorite poet.

So remake your list, and this time don't be attached to those people you love most in the world, but instead really think about who you'd like to spend some time with for your own pleasure, your own enjoyment.

For instance, you might choose one from each of the following:

- A childhood friend

- A favorite poet or artist

- A friend or lover

- A stranger or celebrity

- A teacher or guide

Sure, it's a fantasy—it's your imagination. But what this exercise does is to reach below the surface of what you feel you *ought* to be doing and who you *ought* to be with, to digging for something buried close to your heart.

Now write your "why" list—the list that activates your thinking so that it's in sync with your feeling. Strive for detail. If you've chosen a childhood friend as one of the people you'd most like to spend time with, recall a memory, re-experience the feeling you once had when you were together, and be clear about your expectations of a new encounter.

Listen: *You are always free in your thoughts*

By doing this exercise you're bringing to consciousness deep longings some that may have been hidden for years. You're bringing them out into the light of day, so you can really take a look at them.

They may be less thrilling than they felt when they were hidden at the back of a drawer in your subconscious.

Or your passion for them may well up with an intensity that will not be quelled, no matter what your reason tells you.

What you learn from practicing this exercise, which you're not only going to do once or twice, but over and over, is that you are always free in your thoughts. You can think whatever you want. You can imagine what you want.

You are also free in your feelings. No one has to be trapped in an emotion they choose not to have, though it may take perseverance and hard work to move through it. Being joyful does not just happen—it's a decision you make, and it takes practice. Daily practice.

After a while, you will no longer feel that you are being made to do what you don't want to do because of your conscience, your responsibilities, your boss, your teacher, or your inner parent.

No one makes you feel you have to do anything. No one makes you feel you have to get married or you must be a monk. You make these decisions yourself, and if you don't make them from a place of independent, intuitive *feeling*, you are bound to suffer.

Improvise: *Be brave.*

Say these words: "*I* feel that..." and "*I* want to do..." and "*I* love to..."

Say them out loud.

Louder.

Just don't give up trying to do what you really want to do. Where there is love and inspiration, I don't think you can go wrong. —Ella Fitzgerald

Part II. Feeling

Let us therefore appeal to the balance of Justice, which is at
the same time the balance of peace... Justice is the practical
training of the balance of thinking, feeling, and the will.
                                                   —Meditations on the Tarot

8. Discerning: *Using your head, heart, and hands*

Congratulations. You've unlocked the first seven doors since stepping off the edge of the cliff:

- Effortless concentration.
- Accessing your inner voice.
- Becoming an artist.
- Empowering yourself.
- The initiation of the daily life.
- Being guided by your inner compass.
- Heading off on an adventure.

You're at the point where you need to find an inner *balance* in your travels.

It's a topsy-turvy world, and finding balance within it is not always easy. We tend to live like the swing of a grandfather clock's pendulum: we work, we play. We feel glad—then we feel sad. We think, then we tune out. We swing high, then low. We feel intensely and then we pull back from our emotions.

There is a time for all things, as the great man said, and it is wonderful if you can experience extremes with some sort of equilibrium.

Our greatest power as human beings is that we have the ability

- to feel deeply
- to be conscious of our actions and our feelings—to *think*
- to do, to act.

Most of us tend to be tipped toward one or the other of these three qualities. Some of us are active, practical, doers. Others are passionate, emotional dreamers. Still others are heady intellectuals.

And even the most balanced among us sometimes heads off into a direction of study and thinking, or feels swamped by a morass of emotion, or impulsively charges into a meeting without being prepared. Finding a balance in these three elements that make up every human being is not easy.

Ideally, all three of these qualities are pretty well balanced, though. To be a healthy human being, you need all three in equal measure.

So, practice balance. Whatever you choose today, do it with mindfulness, kindness, and skill. It will make all the difference in your experience of what you do.

I seek within
The working of creative forces,
The life of creative powers.
Earth's gravity is telling me
Through the word of my feet,
Air's wafting forms are telling me
Through the singing of my hands,
And Heaven's light is telling me
Through the thinking of my head,
How the great world in Man
Speaks, sings, and thinks.

—Rudolf Steiner

Practice, Listen, and Improvise

Practice: *Eurythmy*

This practice is based on a little-known art of movement developed in the last century by Rudolf Steiner called "eurythmy." As a Waldorf child, I was taught eurythmy in school as a matter of course from early childhood through my high school graduation, but not many people outside Waldorf Education are aware of the extent of its effectiveness in developing the threefold nature—thinking, feeling, willing—within all of us.

What is eurythmy? It is sound (speech and music) made visible. Paul Klee said, "Art does not reproduce the visible; rather, it makes visible." The art of eurythmy reveals rather than reproduces or interprets. In other words, the movements and gestures made by a eurythmist reveal what is *actually happening* in your larynx or when a note of music is played.

Here are three essential practices from eurythmy that will develop balance in your being.

Developing your will:

Our wonderful feet are three-fold in their structure: toes (head), arch (heart), and heel (will). When you stamp your foot

93

stubbornly, you don't do it on your toes. In this walking meditation, you are going to focus completely on

1. your intention (lifting your heel)
2. your commitment (carrying forward), and
3. your trust (placing).

First, place your feet parallel, the right foot slightly behind the left. All parts of your feet are solid on the ground, your knees slightly bent, equally weighted. Slowly lift your right heel up, as though through water. Arch your foot (not too high) past your left leg, toes pointing down. Place your toes first, then arch, then heel on the ground. You weight has shifted so consciously balance it between both feet again. You have taken a small step, but the step you've taken in inner balancing, in stillness-yet-moving, and in trusting your path are immense.

Now repeat the same process with your left foot.

When you feel you've walked enough, try this same method walking backward. This not only helps with inner and outer balance, but strengthens your trust in your intuition. We live our days putting one foot in front of the other, making decisions, pushing through, setting intentions. Walking backward is a powerful way to learn to trust your inner guide.

Developing your feelings:

In eurythmy, the gestures you make with your hands express every vowel and consonant in speech, and every tone and interval in music. Look at your palm and then look at the back of your hand. Make a fist. Then stretch out your fingers. Imagine the different feelings each of these two gestures creates inside you. This simple activity is an archetypal exercise of contraction and expansion—the essence of your soul's emotional life.

Here's your practice: Place your hands at your breast bone in a fist position but relaxed. Relax your arms and neck and turn your head slightly down. Open your heart by moving your arms out and up. Your fingers will open too, as you stretch your arms wider and wider in an enormous "Y" shape in the air. My eurythmy teacher told me to imagine my arms reaching way past my physical body, past the room, the clouds, the sky, the sun. And then gently travel your hands back into your heart, and bringing them to their relaxed position in which you began.

Developing your thinking:

Your head is a miniature three-fold being, just as your feet are: the forehead, nose, and chin represent thinking, feeling, and willing. You may think that your head doesn't move around much, but it does. Archetypal gestures of the head have been demonstrated in countless studies. For example, young women when they are flirting universally turn slightly to the left and look down, no matter what country or culture they were raised in. Nodding and shaking your head are universal symbols for yes and no. If you look down, with your chin almost touching your chest, this is a gesture of humility, acceptance, or, at the very least, signifies "I don't understand."

One way to develop your awareness of your thoughts is to become conscious of how they are articulated by the gestures of your head. When you move your head, notice that you are doing so. Try this exercise just for a few minutes a day—it's too difficult to do it for long at first.

But if you practice these three exercises for only a short time every day you'll become increasingly aware of your human body as a temple, and also as a microcosm of the universe.

Listen: *What realm do you live in most?*

Do you live mostly in your head or are you an active, 'doing' kind of person? Or are your feelings at the center of your day-to-day existence—do you tend to respond emotionally to events that occur?

Notice which one is hardest for you and which one is the easiest.

We tend to take for granted the kind of person we are, and forget that everyone is different. Honor your own nature, and then work on balancing it. If you feel overwhelmed or exhausted by your emotional response to things, break out of that habit, at least for a while. As soon as emotions begin to take over, do something. Go for a walk. Call a friend. Read a book.

If you're a thinker, go further with a thought you have about something: ask yourself: How does it make you *feel?*

Improvise: *Keep going*

Try to consciously appreciate more things in a three-fold way: thinking, feeling, and doing. Become aware of the times when you get too caught up in one of the three qualities. For instance, in preparing a meal, you need to think about what to cook, you need to cook it, and you need to appreciate it.

Become aware of this in all your activities. Do you spend more time planning than enjoying? Or is the activity the biggest hump?

Notice your responses to even small things that happen during the course of your day.

Do these three practices again, as often as possible. It takes a while for them to become mingled in a real meditative flow. If possible, do it with someone else, or with a group of people. Often, group meditation increases the concentration and commitment.

> *Your hand opens and closes, opens and closes. If it were always a fist or always stretched open, you would be paralyzed. Your deepest presence is in every small contracting and expanding, the two as beautifully balanced and coordinated as birds' wings.* —Rumi

I went to the woods because I wished to live deliberately, to front only the essential facts of life, and see if I could not learn what it had to teach, and not, when I came to die, discover that I had not lived. –Henry David Thoreau

9. Retreating: *Going inward*

One of the most powerful moments in *Parzival*—the story of one of the knights of King Arthur's Round Table—is when he leaves his outward knightly world behind and retreats to live with a Hermit, deep in the woods.

The story is this: Raised by an overly-protective and doting mother, the simple, naïve Parzival is a typically "good" boy. He is courteous, obedient, handsome, and sweet. He is, to a fault, desirous of being liked and so he always does what he is told.

That is, until he encounters a group of knights for the first time. In an instant, he recognizes that his heart's desire is to become a knight himself. His mother, miserable at his insistence on setting off in his slain father's footsteps, dresses him in Fool's clothing, gives him an old, sick horse that cannot travel far, and offers him poor advice that she hopes will have him scurrying back home to her within a matter of days.

Cheerfully, gratefully, but also stubbornly, Parzival kisses her goodbye and sets off.

Parzival passes through many strange adventures, heartbreaks, fearsome battles, and dream-like encounters, before he is given the rare opportunity not only of finding Mumscheavelshe, the vigilantly-guarded castle in which the Grail is hidden, but the Grail itself, that mysterious vessel that is the source of unlimited nourishment to all who are in its presence, and yet causes such grief to those around it.

Unknowingly, he hurts many people, through his naiveté and desire to do the 'right' thing. At the doorway to understanding the mystery of the Grail, he fails to save the Fisher-King from the agony of his terrible wound, because instead of listening to his heart, he listens to other people's advice. When he learns his mistake, he rebelliously disavows knighthood, society, God, and even his beloved wife. He becomes a seeker and retreats into the forest to stay with an old Hermit in the darkest part of the woods. Here he learns deeper truths than mere conventions can teach him: "Know thyself and know the world."

He finally discovers his authentic self.

Many years pass, and as Parzival finds his way toward redemption, he proves himself noble, brave, and loyal. Now, by understanding his true nature and following his own heart, he is able, one by one, to make the wrongs he had committed right again.

By redeeming himself in this way, Parzival is given a rare second chance to ask the Fisher-King the all-important question that will heal his frightful wound and be the salvation of the kingdom.

Written in the twelfth century, the story is set against the great panorama of the Middle Ages, when brave knights wore shining armor and rescued lovely maidens in distress; where castles loomed then disappeared in mysterious gray mists; when vital quests awaited those heroes adventurous enough to seek one; and when the qualities of chivalry, honor, and loyalty warred with desire, greed, and dogma.

The story of Parzival is *your* story—everyone's story. The quest you are on is the quest that life asks of each one of us as we navigate our way through the search for our authentic selves. Obedience to other peoples' insistence on the correct way to do things no longer serves you. Obedience to a dogma, or to knightly rules and regulations, or even to a parent's or spouse's longing to keep you the way you were, will no longer work.

Every action must be made out of the depths of your understanding of your own heart.

Nothing else can guide you in this world besides your own inner compass: not social mores, not parents, not bosses.

So how do you learn to recognize and trust your authentic self?

> *If a man wants to be sure of the road he treads on, he must*
> *close his eyes and walk in the dark.* –Saint John of the Cross

Practice, Listen, and Improvise

Practice: *Meditate*

For this practice you'll need to be alone. Your authentic self is not a mirror of others, nor a projection, nor a persona. It is who you are when you find the deep inner stillness that comes only from being with yourself.

Practice meditation. Meditation is at the core of every spiritual path from time immemorial. It may be called different things in different cultures, but the ability to focus calmly, non-judgmentally, and devotedly on one thing (or no-thing) is essential in your journey.

Meditating instills an equanimity that helps you to feel peaceful even when there are outwardly stressful or urgent situations surrounding you. Instead of getting sucked into an emotional, uncontrollable vortex of fear or anger, you remain calm. Emotions are good—when they're kept in balance.

By meditating, you train your thinking to be intentional, not at the mercy of reaction to others' emergencies. And when you are serene, you help others to be serene as well.

When you are serene, you get a chance to encounter the person you really are.

There are all kinds of ways to practice meditating. You can sit, or whirl, or pray. You can walk, but try not to think. Instead, observe what is around you, without judgment. Focus on your breath if your mind starts wandering. Move through the natural beauty that surrounds you, and observe it with compassionate detachment.

Dancing is another form of meditation—sometimes moving to music helps your mind focus, as on a mantra. It's important to be gentle with yourself. I've known some people to get exasperated with their inability to meditate! The mental chatter that tends to overtake us can be overwhelming. But anyone can find a way to find the quiet stillness of one's innermost being. Be patient. Half the exercise is slowing down, being very still, listening to yourself. Peace doesn't come from somewhere outside—nor does happiness or calm. It comes from going inward.

The practice of meditation trains your mind to be your tool, as opposed to you being the servant of your mind. In life, you can get lost in a dizzying array of stories, ideas, and conversations. You can become dismayed by stress, angst, outside pressures, or "shoulds." Your mind spins tales because that is one of its primary, excellent qualities. But these stories don't need to be in the driver's seat. They can be observed, acknowledged, and gently sent on their way. Meditation shows you the essential usefulness of your mind: it helps you to think, just as your hands help you write and your feet help you walk. Your mind is not your self. Your mind is useful—but it needs to learn how to be still and quiet to make room for creativity and calm.

If you haven't meditated before—or only rarely or with a teacher—here are basic instructions for beginning:

Find a place where you know you won't be interrupted. Be comfortably seated. Close your eyes. For five or so minutes, focus on your breath. You'll sense it going in and out, and you might get twitchy and bored and begin to think of something else. Gently focus your mind back on your breathing.

After five minutes, gently let go of your concentration and open your eyes.

That's it.

Over the course of the next days or weeks, increase your meditating time to ten, then fifteen, then twenty minutes. Eventually you'll find the time that works best for you. Transcendental meditation recommends twenty minutes twice a day. Za-zen monks meditate for seven or eight hours at a time.

If you already know how to meditate, but do it only on occasion, try to practice it regularly for a week and observe any changes.

If you're a seasoned meditator, then try a different kind of meditation for a week or two, to stretch and flex your meditation muscles. There are so many varieties to choose from—focusing on a mantra, moving meditation, walking, dancing, whirling, breathing, emptiness.

Listen: *Journal*

After each meditation, take five minutes or so to write down your experience. There are two reasons writing is important. The first is that, like Parzival entering the Hermit's cave, as you meditate, areas deep inside yourself may begin to be uncovered— things you didn't know about yourself, for instance—and you want to record this. You may not always remember some rare insight, clear as it may seem right after your meditation. Also in the process of writing, new insights may come to you.

Improvise: *Where did I come from? Who am I? Where am I going?*

After free writing, these are the questions you'll want to ponder:

Where did I come from?

When you write an answer to this (and try to do it after each meditation session) begin from where you are now and go backward. You can soar or float through the imaginings—don't get caught up in detail. For instance, you might write something like:

Moved to Iowa—had kids—second marriage—the ice cream factory—left college—high school prom—traveled south ...

Just the bare outline going back as far as you can remember.

Each day add some small detail—at least one feeling for each event that you remember. Just words like "sad" or "anxious" or "so happy." And try to remember farther back. If you have an idea of a memory from so long ago you don't even know if you made it up—including a 'feeling' you think might be from a past life—trust it. Include it. Your imagination knows more than you think!

Do this for a week, rounding out your biography from the present to the beginning.

The second part of this exercise is to answer the question:

Who Am I?

After each meditation, write some words about yourself. Perhaps ten words will come, perhaps twenty. Don't worry if the words or phrases are repetitious the first few days. More will come.

Before going on to the third and final phase of this practice, get a large sheet of square paper and put a dot in its center. Draw a circle around this dot, leaving plenty of room beyond the outer circumference. Right in between the dot and the outer circle, draw another circle.

Within the smallest circle write the words and phrases that you have repeated most often in answer to your first question "Where did I come from?"

In the next circle, freely and having fun with the process, write in the words and phrases you've been writing over the past week that describe you.

Use colored pencils if you like, or include doodles. You can make this as beautiful or as workmanlike as you want.

Study your diagram.

After your meditation practice look at it, and get a sense of yourself as an expanding ball rather than as a line that's being drawn from A to B.

Now you're ready to do your final exercise:

Where am I going?

The question is not yet *What would I do if there was nothing I had to do*, because you want to assimilate all the essences that are you first and really understand yourself. Know yourself first. Where are you going? How does your future appear to you?

So meditate, and empty yourself of the expectations, and nervousness, or excitement you might be preparing for in your future. When you're done, write some words and phrases on the outside circumference about where you think you are headed.

You can be dry and clear—promotion, family, retirement, relocating. You can also think about your emotional life: "I will be calmer. More patient. Assertive.

But after a few days you'll want to begin to write your longings and dreams here too. Where would you go if you could go anywhere? You have your whole life expanding outward like a beautiful golden ball—and only infinity to expand into. Don't let your dreams be limited by your idea of constraints. Free yourself up to imagine your life as wildly, crazily, fabulously ideal.

It's not what you call me, but what I answer to. –African proverb

⊷

Forces beyond your control can take away everything you possess except one thing: your freedom to choose how you will respond to the situation.
—*Viktor Frankl*

10. Responding: *Destiny and luck*

The most difficult time to be true to yourself is when unexpected things turn up, blocking your way or veering you off course. That's life, too. The wheel of fortune does turn, the three Fates continue to weave the fabric of your life, and sometimes it is not in a pattern that you feel comfortable with.

What do you do when you find yourself in a situation that surprises, upsets, or wrestles you to the ground? How can you remain true to yourself if you're having to deal with something that's come at you seemingly out of the blue and not at all what you had planned or prepared for?

How can you look at your destiny and see patterns or recognize insights? What about past lives, luck, karma, and the cycles of birth, marriage, death? What about your daily life?

If you've worked on the practices so far, you understand how to be guided by your inner compass. You understand that staying true to yourself will help you to rise above the tumult of life.

And the essential truth is that although you cannot control the wheel of fortune, you can *always* control the way you deal with being on the wheel. When mystics talk about free will and the fact that "the stars indicate, they do not compel," *this* is what they mean. Your future is based not on the event that occurs but on *how you respond to it.*

Nelson Mandela was jailed for twenty-eight years for speaking out against the law of apartheid, and by the time he was finally released, his jailers were so inspired by his dignity, courage, respectfulness, and kindness that they had become his most loyal supporters. As president, he urged a country to move into a new era through forgiveness and reconciliation rather than revenge and punishment for the atrocities that had occurred.

Another inspiring and moving story is that of Azim Noordin Khamisa. After his son was murdered, Azim made the decision to dedicate his life to trying to break the cycle of violence against children around the world. As Phil Cousineau describes in *Beyond Forgiveness:* "Azim's message combines the virtues and morality of forgiveness with the compassion and humility of atonement, which includes reaching out to others who have also lost loved ones to violence."

Not many of us are called upon to lead a country or rebuild a shattered existence, but these role models of ways to respond to atrocity or grief are still lessons to us all in our daily lives.

How you respond to a situation makes all the difference to its outcome.

I had a neighbor, for instance, who refused to talk to me, meet my eye, or even wave from across the street. I must have done something to offend her, but to this day I don't know what that is. I tried asking, but was rebuffed. At first I was shocked and hurt when she simply glared at me and walked past. For a while I avoided being anywhere around if she was going in or out of her driveway.

After a while, I gradually came to realize her attitude was about her, not me. I could respond to her hostility in any way I wanted to, and the outcome of our relationship would change! Even if she never changed in her attitude toward me, I would release the shock and hurt, and *be myself*. I'm a friendly person, I like to smile and wave to my neighbors. I think it's courteous. So I decided to remain true to myself, and from then on I always smiled at her when I saw her.

To my surprise, after a few years, she began smiling back. We never really spoke, and certainly never became friends, but I wasn't quelled into fear and dislike by her attitude toward me. I smiled; eventually she smiled.

We were neighbors.

It is not what happens to you that counts—it's how you respond. Your response to your life is your path to human freedom.

> *I knew that in finding the mandala as an expression of the self*
> *I had attained what was for me the ultimate.* —C. G. Jung

Practice, Listen, and Improvise

Practice: *Create a mandala*

In Sanskrit, the word *mandala* literally means a circle. As you create your mandala, imagine your conscious self is in the center, the middle circle is your personal unconscious, and the collective unconscious is on the periphery.

All the designs and shapes around the center are connected and interrelated.

You'll need:

- paper and pencil
- a ruler
- a compass
- colors (watercolor paints or colored pencils—whatever you enjoy using. (I advise against magic markers or anything inorganic: the chemicals, smells, and fake vibrancy won't serve you as well as authentic sources of color.)

Cut your paper into a square.

Using your ruler to measure the sides of the square, draw two lines, one that is horizontal across the page and the other one straight up and down, that cross each other right in the middle, dividing your page into four sections.

You've made your center dot.

Using your compass, draw a series of circles around this dot. You can make as few as three circles or as many as you'd like.

Draw an X shape so that the circle is divided into eight sections.

Begin by drawing a simple geometric pattern in one section of your mandala. Now repeat that same design in each of the other sections. The repeating patterns are key to experiencing the mandala as a tool for self-development, and it is important to create each design in each section before you go on to the next one.

Mandalas are used in cultures all over the world to aid self-development. Alchemists refer to the mandala as a "sacred wheel." It's a wheel because your journey to self-knowledge never ends, but as you circle around again you can see where you have been. The journey is dynamic and transforming.

In the alchemical journey, the mandala is based on the four elements. The stage of earth is followed by water, which is followed by air, and then by fire. Then you come back to earth.

This pattern is based on the laws of nature: earth on the bottom, water above it, air above that, and fire on top.

Dennis Klocek, in *The Seer's Handbook*, describes it this way: "When an alchemist starts to work on him/herself this beginning stage is known as putting the fire under the earth. When putting the fire under the earth the alchemist is working against the natural order of things or working against nature. To cook a meal is working against nature according to alchemy. To cook my beliefs about myself is to change my unconscious patterns in my life that are not working for me. Changing my unconscious patterns is also a work against nature. In this important work I learn to overcome the things that are holding me back from reaching my goals in life."

Take your time. You can use as many colors as you choose and incorporate as many designs as you'd like. You can start from the center and move outward, or start in the middle circles or on the periphery.

A mandala becomes a reflection of your soul. You explore shapes and colors that represent anything from frustration to deeply held longings you've kept buried.

By designing your own mandala, you discover a sense of self and your place in the world. You can do this in whatever way you wish, and you may find the practice is one you want to repeat over and over, using new themes or designs.

Your mandala can be drawn using both geometric and organic forms. It doesn't have to be abstract: Use imagery that has meaning for you. The idea is that it will represent the connection between your inner and outer worlds.

Listen: *Meditate*

Meditate on your mandala. Do this for at least five minutes every day.

As you meditate on your mandala, you'll experience a growing connection with your authentic self. According to Jung, our need to become ourselves is as real and intense as every organism's compulsion to manifest what is characteristic of its own nature.

Improvise: *Create more mandalas*

Create more mandalas based on feelings or ideas that you want to explore more deeply. Be inventive. Use shapes in nature that have meaning to you, like a flower or a tree. Or rocks or mineral shapes. Perhaps mazes have intrigued you for a long time or sailors' knots. The artist Sarah Nicholson is celebrated for her highly original photographs of women's vaginas which she then creates into mandalas for them to meditate on. Choose motifs that intrigue you—trust that you are attracted to those motifs for a reason.

Going inward and then outward, even symbolically, will flex your connection to your authentic self.

> *Within the circle of a perfect one there is an infinite community of light.*
> —Hafiz

Fear is only as deep as the mind allows. —Japanese proverb

11. Encouraging: *You're braver than you think*

It's okay to be afraid.

But it's not okay to let that stop you from doing something you want or need to do.

When I think about fear, on whatever level—even if it's dreading having to pick up the phone to make a call—I am reminded of the Cowardly Lion in *The Wizard of Oz*. That fabulous, warm-hearted lion plunged into every terrifying situation with his whole heart, saving Dorothy and his friends over and over, in spite of the fact that he was terrified every time.

He could not have been brave if he was not afraid.

In *Feel the Fear and Do It Anyway*, Susan Jeffers tells us that it is not the activity of something that frightens us, it is the idea that we can't handle it. And the idea that we can't handle it is typically ingrained deeply within us. As she says, how often will a mother say to her child as he goes off to school, "Take lots of risks today, honey"? More likely it's "Be careful."

"Drive carefully."

"Take care."

There is great courage in being able to admit that you are afraid. It takes courage to be vulnerable. Not the "poor me" that begs for sympathy, but the "oh my god—I can't do this alone" kind of vulnerability, that inspires others to reach out and hug you or take your hand to help you along.

You are part of a world of human beings and we are all connected. What other people have accomplished gives you strength just as what you accomplish strengthens other people.

When you do triumph over a fear, that inward success ripples out into the world with a profound effect. Each time you meet a challenge, overcome a weakness, or pick someone up and dust them off, you accomplish something that affects other people.

So be brave—because it makes an enormous difference to us all. Most importantly, though, it makes a difference in your quest to live the life you really want to live. It takes courage to look someone in the eye and tell them something they don't want to hear because you want them to make a change, for their own sake.

It takes even more courage to look inside yourself and do the same thing.

You risked your life, but what else have you ever risked? Have you risked disapproval? Have you ever risked economic security? Have you ever risked a belief? I see nothing particularly courageous about risking one's life. So you lose it, you go to your hero's heaven and everything is milk and honey 'til the end of time. Right? You get your reward and suffer no earthly consequences. That's not courage. Real courage is risking something that might force you to rethink your thoughts and suffer change and stretch consciousness. Real courage is risking one's clichés. —Tom Robbins

Practice, Listen, and Improvise

Practice: *Risk disapproval*

Choose something in your life that you wish you could change or speak up about, but you just haven't bothered to, or you've been too tired, or you're afraid to.

This could be as simple as telling a friend something about yourself you know she'd disapprove of, or refusing to go to a relative's house for a function you're dreading.

Tell your boss you're not going to bring that cup of coffee.

Walk into a high-end store that has always intimidated you and trying on lots of clothes.

Present an opposing point of view to your spouse or parent.

You don't have to argue or stand up for yourself or be quelled. You just need to present yourself as the person you really are. There's no reason to keep your light hidden under a bushel.

Stand up for yourself. Are you in the middle of painting and you're being asked to stop to make dinner? Smile, wave, and say, "Sorry, honey, I'm busy. Please take care of it."

Or perhaps a friend wants to see a movie that repels you, but you promised you'd go. Tell her you've changed your mind.

If you can choose one thing to stand up for each day, the courage inside you will grow stronger. The process is not subtle— it's powerful. The courage within grows exponentially, as you realize that asking someone else to take care of making dinner is not going to end the world and that your friend still loves you even if you don't want to see that particular movie.

By standing up for yourself, you are also holding up a mirror for others to see themselves. It is one of the great gifts you can offer to others, as well as to yourself.

Listen: *Write your response*

This is a tremendous opportunity for you to face your insecurity, pride, fear or distrust of your emotions, your inner power struggles, your stubbornness, integrity, determination, drama, and any sort of prejudices or rages that are a part of your shadow side, and that you have kept buried.

By doing this exercise you realize that you can handle whatever happens. Unpleasantness, argument, or pressure may not feel blissful, but *the world does not come to an end if you say no!*

Write down your difficult experiences and always include your emotional response to them.

Then your task is to act with courage.

Improvise: *Risk your beliefs*

Risk a spiritual belief or any dogma you are attached to. Imagine believing something you think you can't. If you're an atheist, for example, try imagining a profound faith in God. If you are devoutly religious, take a day living every moment as though you are an atheist. Look at everything from a materialistic viewpoint. Or imagine yourself a pagan, and see divinity in nature.

Risk a political belief. Find an aspect of an opposing political viewpoint that resonates. Go deeper, and imagine yourself standing up for something that normally disturbs you. When you look at your own political belief, examine it through the eyes of the opposition. Tear it up, analyze, scrutinize. See its negative aspects and its problems.

Risk an emotional belief. This is one of the hardest beliefs to risk. Emotions often are so deeply ingrained in us that we don't even realize they are beliefs—we think they're 'true.'

For instance, when we marry we promise to stay together "in sickness and health." For many of us, this means when our spouse gets sick or is terminally ill, it's our duty to be sole caregiver. It is hard to shift that belief so that we also rely on family members, friends, social services, and other support systems to share responsibility.

Or here's another example: My husband hates to travel. We both work at home, our ideal lifestyle choice. However, I also like to go places. For many years I felt unable to go places or visit faraway friends simply because *he* didn't want to. If I'd been asked, I would not have realized this was the case. I would have believed that I was choosing to stay at home—perhaps to save money, or because I liked being with him so much, or for the sake of my children. But looking back I realize I was a prisoner of a belief in those three reasons not to travel. My heart's desire was to go away sometimes. It's taken many years of practicing standing up for myself to turn some of my beliefs on their heads.

You are always free in your thoughts, but not if you let yourself become a prisoner of even one of them.

Standing up for yourself guides you to a place where you can make peace with yourself, not just with others. You align all the shadowy parts of your nature with strength, courage, and, ultimately, the tenderness of your heart.

This exercise will help you to align your courage with your passion. You'll be able to sift out what your heart desires from what you've been raised to believe it "should" desire.

You'll have the courage and confidence to stand up for that heart's desire.

The desire for safety stands against every great and noble enterprise. –Tacitus

\

Acceptance will be the essence coming; it will be like a benediction, a blessing, a gentle rain...When that surrender to the truth happens, then acceptance comes and is experienced as a gentle, cool shower. –A. H. Almaas

12. Surrendering: *Having patience*

L et it go.

Whether you are surrendering to suffering or to inheriting a splendid fortune, sometimes it's out of your hands. Look at your situation differently, and realize sometimes patience and acceptance are more effective than a more active response. "Do nothing" as a practice of surrender. And if you have to do something, do it mindfully.

Let go of your suffering.

Learn to tread lightly over those aspects of your life that you feel most constrained by. Regard them as bubbles or feathers. In some respect, you really have chosen the situation, even if it's one that you wish was different.

Learn from it. Respond to it with as much levity, serenity, and kindness toward yourself as you can.

> *People have a hard time letting go of their suffering. Out of a fear of the unknown, they prefer suffering that is familiar.* –Thich Nhat Hanh

Practice, Listen, and Improvise

Practice: *Letting go*

Examine a part of your life over which you have no control.

Take a piece of paper and write the situation down at the top. Then divide the page into three columns.

In the first column write down all the reasons there is nothing you can do about the situation. For example, if you are stuck in a job that is debilitating, boring, abusive, or stressful, write down why you believe you have to stay there.

Get as detailed as possible. If there is absolutely no opportunity for a different job, write down why not. If your relationship with your boss or a co-worker is hopelessly unbearable, write down why it can never—*in your mind*—change.

If it is caregiving an elderly parent, write down your reasons why you are the only source of support. Include finances, health care, guilt, siblings—*everything*.

In the middle column write your feelings about each reason that keeps you in that situation. Be brutally honest. Putting your feelings outside yourself, in a list, stops those emotions from coursing around in your head where they can confuse you and prevent you from thinking clearly.

Now write a third column that describes all the positive qualities to the situation. You'll find that some are duplicated from the first column. Income, for example, or affection, or wanting to improve a child's experience.

You may also find some of the positive qualities are the flip side of the negative ones. For example, a negative aspect of a job responsibility may be that you have to travel a lot and you miss your family. A positive one may be that you love to travel.

Seeing a situation in black and white on a page like this lessens its power over you.

Mull over your three columns by releasing all your impatience, fear, or frustration. Instead, try to experience a feeling of trust that what you are doing is what has to be done. Don't be judgmental or critical or let yourself feel hopeless. Simply observe the situation as though you were an objective, compassionate witness.

Surrender to what is.

The power of surrender cannot be over-estimated. It is one of our greatest tools we can use to experience deep inner peace. Complete surrender leads to self-transformation, and from transformation, to a new self-direction.

Do this this for as many situations as you can that you feel are out of your control or holding you back from realizing your dream.

Listen: *Serenity prayer*

Memorize the serenity prayer and repeat it to yourself over and over:

> God grant me the serenity
> to accept the things I cannot change;
> courage to change the things I can;
> and wisdom to know the difference.

Improvise: *Forgiving*

When you forgive, do you forgive the act, or the person, or yourself for having to forgive in the first place? If you feel remorse, is that enough? Or if someone else forgives you, but you don't forgive yourself, does that make it okay?

I think that in many ways forgiveness comes from a different place, not a human one. Our job is to get out of the way *so that forgiveness can happen.*

Not long before my mother died, she read Phil Cousineau's book called *Beyond Forgiveness.* He writes about a process of "atonement": making amends, providing restitution, and restoring balance.

She was powerfully moved by how so many human beings have been able to move through incredible tragedy and suffering to reach a place of atonement and reconciliation. And she herself did not want to die if she had not atoned in some way for any hurt she may have caused, no matter how small. When I visited, she would ask me, "Is there anything we need to talk about? Work out together? Are we okay—you and me?"

Each time I assured her we were absolutely, one hundred percent, totally, completely okay. Her expression of relief and love is one of my happiest memories.

Write a list of people you find hard to forgive for some reason. Then write down what would allow you to forgive them. Sometimes it's no more than a simple "sorry."

Now write a list describing things you have done that you find hard to forgive. Mull over what could change that stuck feeling. Sometimes the mere act of writing it down-shifts it from being an area you can hardly bear to look at to something barely significant.

If you have enormous guilt, strategize a way to move toward atonement.

The strategy that works the best is *to get out of the way*, and let forgiveness happen.

> *You are*
> *A royal fish*
> *Trying to wear pants*
> *In a country as foreign*
> *As land.*
>
> ...
>
> *Why*
> *Be a royal fish*
> *Trying to wear pants?*
>
> —Hafiz

*Death is a stripping away of all that is not you. The secret of life is to "die
before you die" and find that there is no death.* –Eckhart Tolle

13. Transforming: *The cycle of nature*

The cycles of life and death are cycles of transformation. In
the process of discovering your essential self and re-
making your life, you are either going to have to leave
behind that which is no longer necessary—whether a
relationship, a house, or a body—or transform it into something
new.

The process can be painful. We tend to be attached to what is
familiar and safe. We cling to dead wood as though we might
drown without it, even if there is a sturdy lifeboat nearby.

If you can transform your fear of change and the unknown, into feelings of relief and release, you can make great leaps forward in your journey.

The dying process is going to happen to you, *whether you want it to or not*. Children *do* grow up and leave. Parents do die. You may lose your job. You do have to throw out a worn-out shirt you loved. A friend does move. It's how you respond to these events that makes the difference.

Are you going to resist and moan and groan and gnash your teeth at the unfairness of it all? Or are you going to recognize that an experience, relationship, job, work, apartment has outlived its usefulness to you and gratefully and gracefully move on?

Each time you experience a small death—really letting something die inside you and releasing it—you also experience a rebirth of your inner self. Each time it happens you are stronger, more confident, even *happier*, in spite of the outward appearance of loss.

You *have* to let go of things that no longer serve you. At a certain time, winter does move into spring. It's not just the death of winter—it's the birth of spring.

And summer does follow. And then the roses *do* die.

Again.

Accept the end of something—perhaps even something you loved or still love dearly—in order to allow something new to enter your life.

Death is not extinguishing the light; it is only putting out the lamp because the dawn has come. –Rabindranath Tagore

Practice, Listen, and Improvise

Practice: *Seeing death as a part of nature*

It's not easy to fully accept the fact that something is *Over*.

Done.

Finished.

Do you still have a lingering feeling of "something more you have to do" in your life? How can you release even that?

How do you know when it's time to move on?

One way is to become aware of the cycles of life and death in nature. I have found this to be one of the most healing and natural ways to become increasingly grateful and graceful through the dying/transforming process.

In nature this process happens all the time, so much so that we hardly recognize the life cycle that surrounds us constantly includes experiences of dying and death.

In ancient times people learned to cope with living and dying through festival and ceremony. But this is something largely lost in our present-day cultures. We equate festivals with street fairs, vendors, and commercialism; and ceremonies are confused with religion or dogma.

But if you go reach deeply into your humanity, you'll realize that your natural life—the life experienced in and about and around Nature—is as much a part of you as breathing.

Festivals used to be inextricably tied to the rhythms of life and death, sowing and reaping, seasons, and the circling of the stars and planets. If you can tap into that source, you will find that the process of letting go gets easier and easier, because you begin to recognize not just the transience of life, but its constant regeneration.

Learn about some ancient festivals that were based on natural law, connected in some way to the process of transformation—from death, to transformation, to rebirth. Everything in nature reflects this process and even festivals that appear on the surface to stem from religious ideology were usually founded on pagan or agricultural rituals from ancient times.

Each culture is unique and celebrates in different ways. You are part of the culture you were born into, and you belong to the community in which you live. Find out about what has resonated around you for centuries and how the cycles of life and death and rebirth have impacted generations around you.

We are individuals, yes. But we are physical beings, and we are part of our surroundings and the people around us. Becoming aware of your community and discovering its natural rhythms, and finding some that bring you joy, will help you in this time of transformation. You need to find your place in nature, as a natural human being.

For example, the Celtic festival known as Beltane is one rarely celebrated anymore. It falls on the first day of May, at the height of spring. Bel is the Celtic god of light, and in the northern hemisphere it is at this time of the year that the light is strongest. The farther north you go, the longer the twilight—that murky, dim, silvery brilliance that imbues the world till late into the night.

In ancient times, when people were closely connected to the rhythm of the seasons, on the eve of Beltane, they lit bonfires to Bel to call back the sun. They jumped over the fires to purify ourselves, and they blessed their all-important animals by leading them from winter barns to summer pastures between those bonfires. Celebrations were filled with merriment—dancing, tournaments, feasting, and love-making. Flowers were abundant and even the mysterious Green Man was sometimes visible.

At the school I went to in Sussex, England, we left baskets anonymously on the door step of an elderly or unwell neighbor on the first of May. Girls woke up before dawn and we bathed our faces in the dew (although it was usually soft rain). We danced around a maypole, the girls wearing wreaths and garlands and the boys covered (or so it seemed) in bells. At the end of the complex, varied, joyous dancing, we braided the maypole with the colorful ribbons.

Tane means fire and Beltane was the celebration of Light and Fire. This is the time of year when the energy of the earth and our bodies is the strongest. Fiery Aries has moved into earthy Taurus and if you're friends with a farmer, you'll rarely find them socializing now—there is so much work to be done. We're now into the summer half of the year, a time when the sun rises early and sets late, and when everything is growing with great energy.

There are good reasons for the Druids to honor the sun above all else: The sun is our earth's heart. It beats at this time of year with the most passion. It is in love with the earth and with the people on it. Take off your hat at sunrise and sunset, as the people of the Highlands in Scotland used to do, in honor and appreciation of our magnificent Sun.

The quickening life forces of this time of year are most evident in the newborn lambs, bear cubs, and kid goats, and a general sense of new birth. Listen to the birds outside your window: it seems as though they are chirping and trilling for sheer joy. Beltane epitomizes love and making love. In days long ago, if you weren't already pregnant, this was when you and your lover would wander to the green wood and spend the night in a bower to make love.

If you want to try to see the spirits, wait till late in the evening, then bend a rowan or willow branch into a ring and gaze through it. This takes patience and practice.

Or make a Maibowle of fruity May wine and celebrate spirits that way. May wine used to be made with fragrant woodruff flavoring sweet white wine—but you can use any fresh fruit juice and soak violets, pansies, nasturtiums, or other edible blossoms in it.

Listen: *Festival life*

Create a ceremony around something in your life that has been somewhat burdensome. This is best done in a group, if possible, with people who understand what you are trying to accomplish.

Be specific about the ritual, the attendees, the place, and—most important—the purpose.

You can choose to create a ceremony around the loss of a job, or the clearing of a closet. Our traditional ceremonies (memorials, birthdays, anniversaries) are fine; but dig deeper. One woman I know felt the onset of menopause to be like a death—the death of her fertility and womanhood. By creating a ritual around this, we were able to help her transform her sadness into a new vision of herself as a woman—one no less womanly than during her fertile years.

If you've had to move recently, or even if you want to regenerate your relationship to your house, try creating a house festival. Use singing bowls, rattles, drums, candles, smudge sticks, chanting... do what feels right. Tie ribbons on the windows. Dance between the doors.

Here are more activities to inspire your ceremony or festival: Wander to a stream or lake—or the ocean—and bless the water spirits or ask for their blessing. Listen and listen even more: the cycles of life begin to permeate your being like sparkling ripples in a stream that meanders through a meadow. Light a candle and jump over it (symbol of the great bonfire of Beltane—do this with attention and care).

Or, if you have a small garden, or even a window box, or if you live on the edge of the woods, keep in mind that—like Samhain in the middle of autumn—Beltane is the time of the year when the veil between this world and the invisible world is thin and can be parted. This is when you might see or sense fairies, elves, or other elemental beings—spirits who surround us even if you can't see them.

Liken your experience to that of a caterpillar becoming a moth: preparation—death (of the cocoon)—transformation—rebirth.

Make your festival *fun*—as joyous as you can, no matter how poignant or deeply moving the letting go is for you.

Improvise: *Be in nature as much as possible*

Become increasingly aware of the natural world around you. Really get a sense for the life pouring through a tree or a field of goldenrod. Grow quiet and let the natural spirits approach.

With practice, you might even be lucky enough to experience elemental beings. My grandmother was the first person who told me about elementals. She described them as creatures who worked hard to keep the elements (fire, earth, air, and water) from getting too dense, literally enlivening the elements for us so we can live on earth.

One day she told me about some rain goblins she'd seen. She described them as about eight inches high, skinny, wrinkled, brown-skinned, and rather leaping in spirit. Her description was so detailed and vivid that I knew without a doubt she actually had seen these creatures.

Imagine being in your garden, or taking a walk in the woods, from the point of view of an elemental being. Try to get into the spirit of this being. A dryad, or tree nymph, will have a tree-like spirit, rooted in the ground and swaying in a breeze. Water creatures tend toward travel and adventure. Fire spirits move quickly and exude sparkle and light—what kind of picture would they have of our world? What are earth creatures, like elves and goblins, really like?

Even if you can't actually see an elemental being, as my grandmother could, try to imagine their characteristics, and their helpfulness in bringing light to the density of our physical beings. Bring in all the wisdom you can imagine such an elemental creature has garnered through millennia.

This practice will help you attain a feeling of equanimity as you experience the daily, yearly, and inevitable 'final' death each one of us experiences throughout our lives and without which we could not live.

This existence of ours is as transient as autumn clouds. To watch the birth and death of being is like looking at the movements of a dance. A lifetime is like a flash of lightning in the sky. Rushing by, like a torrent down a steep mountain.
–Buddha

⊖—⊤

To be calm is the highest achievement of self. –Zen proverb

14. Being calm: *The gift of equanimity*

One day I ordered a cup of Yogi tea and the little tag on the teabag had this saying: "To be calm is the highest achievement of self."

At first I was taken aback. All I had to do to achieve the wisdom of selfhood was to be calm? It seemed much too easy!

But it is not.

Another word for calm is equanimity or, in the language of the tarot, temperance. Through equanimity you learn that your life can achieve its own harmony, regardless of the storms raging around. By maintaining a balance, by mindfully pouring from the cup of the heart into the cup of the mind and back again, you attain an inner calm that ennobles and empowers you immeasurably.

Equanimity is one of the most satisfying feelings in the world— even more delightful than bliss or ecstasy, because you can remain in this state forever. Tranquility, meeting disaster with calm, serenity, and the realization that whatever happens, you can handle it, brings you an astounding freedom.

Equanimity means balance in action, harmony, co-operation in relationships, living in the moment, contentment, flow. *"People are born for different tasks, but in order to survive every one requires the same nourishment: inner peace."*–Sri Sathya Sai Baba

This is your opportunity to take a look back over your journey so far. You have taken thirteen enormous leaps forward. Every one of them has built on the previous one, and by the time you arrive at this stage of equanimity, you have all the tools necessary to help you attain it.

Start by taking a look back at who you were at the beginning of this journey. Reconnect with that brave Fool who took the first step off the edge of a cliff.

Calmness is one of the attributes of the immortality within you....When you worry, there is static coming through your mind radio. God's song is the song of calmness. Nervousness is the static; calmness is the voice of God speaking to you through the radio of your soul. —Paramahansa Yogananda

Practice, Listen, and Improvise

Practice: *13 ways of being calm*

1. *Breathe. Go with the flow.* Remember the juggling exercise, when you learned how to do an activity with effortless concentration? Well, you may not always have your juggling balls with you to bring you levity and flow, but here's something that is even easier: When you feel your calm slipping away, bring your attention to your breathing in the same way you used to focus on your juggling. Deep, slow

breathing physically calms you down by bringing oxygen to your brain, by activating the hypothalamus. This is connected to the pituitary gland in the brain, which sends out neurohormones that inhibit stress-producing hormones and at the same time relax you.

Here's how: place your hands on your belly, so you can actually see your tummy rise and fall. That way you know you're breathing deeply enough. Breathe through your nose; and take even lengths of inhales and exhales. Take a tiny but conscious rest between each breath.

2. *Trust your intuition.* Trying to figure something out in your head can drive you nuts. Sometimes your mind just goes around in circles and a problem or emotion takes on a life of its own, one that spins of its own accord and that you can't seem to stop. This especially happens in the middle of the night, as anyone who has woken up with an anxious start at two a.m. knows. Instead, try to listen to your subconscious. Let your inner voice be your guide.

    One way to still the relentless anxious voices is to write down the problem. Seeing it in black and white on a piece of paper distances you from it, so it doesn't seem enmeshed in you, but rather becomes a separate issue that has to be solved. By separating it from you, you'll be freer to listen to your inner voice. Sometimes you don't even hear the voice— you just put one foot in front of the other because you know it's the right thing to do. But you *are* calmer as you take those steps.

3. *Create.* Doing something artistic is relaxing. If you don't have the time or energy to calm yourself by going into the woods and writing a poem, then listen to calming music, or spend an hour in a museum looking at just one painting.

4. *Empower yourself.* You have the power to control what goes on inside you, even if you don't have the power to control a situation that is outside you. Go inward, and grow aware of your inner calm. Remind yourself that you are in control of

yourself. By empowering yourself in this way, you'll remember that *you are in charge of your own feelings.*

5. *Find a ritual.* When your calm is ruffled, make sure you have some sort of a ritual you can fall on that will bring balance to the situation. It can be as simple as taking a walk, drawing a quick mandala, reading a beloved poem, or lighting a candle.

6. *Choose wisely.* Don't feel you have to engage in every battle or climb onto someone else's emotional rollercoaster. Decide what you want t or can deal with, and if it's going to drain you or make you miserable, refuse to engage. Give yourself a break.

7. *Slow down.* Remember *Even Cowgirls Get the Blues*, by Tom Robbins? Here's something from it: *You've heard of people calling in sick. You may have called in sick a few times yourself. But have you ever thought about calling in well? It'd go like this: You'd get the boss on the line and say, "Listen, I've been sick ever since I started working here, but today I'm well and I won't be in anymore." Call in well.*

8. *Decide what matters.* Avoid situations and people who irritate or anger you. If hot weather bothers you, go to an air-conditioned movie. Don't let yourself get too hungry... and try to get enough sleep. Think about what matters to you. Ask yourself "Is it vital?"

9. *Retreat...* practice meditation. How about a quiet walking meditation? Breathe naturally to the rhythm of your pace and observe what is around you with compassionate, but neutral, objectivity.

10. *Practice responding with calm and dignity.* The only thing you really are in control of in your life is how you respond to any given situation.

11. *You're braver than you think.* Move through difficult situations by placing one foot in front of the other—with confidence, courage, skill.

12. *Surrender.* Let other people take charge sometimes. Listen to them without feeling you have to change them or change the situation. Let go of responsibility, control, stress.

13. There is little that is more calming and reassuring than observing the cycles of life—death transformation—and rebirth.

So, practice being calm. You have learned how by passing through the thirteen stages you have experienced so far.

Listen: *Be kind to yourself*

Stop putting yourself down with negative self-talk. Respect your talents, beauty, your strengths and your challenges. Appreciate them with all your heart.

One way to do this is to imagine yourself as a young child, one you love passionately. Even if a child is messy, loud, or tantrummy, you adore her or him. Imagine your soul as a beloved child and love yourself unconditionally, with a love that inspires tranquility and peace in your heart.

Consciously putting an end to inner chattering that puts you down or threatens you or discourages you takes a lot of practice.

Tie a length of string around your wrist and every time something negative about yourself crosses your mind or passes your lips, tie another knot in it. You might be surprised how many knots you'll find at the end of the day. By becoming conscious of them, you'll gradually recognize their appearance and gently dismiss them *before* they begin their chatter.

Improvise

Other tips:

Sleep: Essential. You know how strung out and stressed you feel if you haven't had a good night's sleep. Get more of it. And even more.

Exercise. Exercising is not only great for your physical body, but it calms your mind. When you exercise, endorphins start playing around in your brain and lighten your mood and mental well-being. Even a short walk makes a huge difference.

Nutrition: Eat and drink well, lightly, using fresh, organic, wholesome ingredients. Processed foods and the chemicals used to process them make you feel physically (and therefore mentally) agitated. You can eat and drink anything you like—always in moderation—as long as it's healthy.

Optimism. You can decide to be optimistic. It is more of a decision than a personality. Everything can be looked at in a positive light. And looking at things from a positive perspective brings feelings of peace and calm.

Mantra: Repeat the words "be calm" or "all is well" or any other verbal reminder in a stressful or negative situation.

Feel your emotions. You can feel strong emotions even while you are calm. You can be sure Gandhi was passionately emotional about justice and freedom. So was Martin Luther King, whose passion for his cause resonated through every word he uttered. And yet he remained calm in the face of the worst situations imaginable. You don't need to hold in or repress your emotions. Crying can bring an extraordinary calm afterward, for instance.

Friends, don't gloss over these tips for feeling calm because they seem to be clichés you have heard too many times. Go through each one and absorb it into your life. *Choose* to live calmly.

Responsibility does not only lie with the leaders of our countries or with those who have been appointed or elected to do a particular job. It lies with each of us individually. Peace, for example, starts within each one of us. When we have inner peace, we can be at peace with those around us. When our community is in a state of peace, it can share that peace with neighboring communities, and so on. —Dalai Lama

Part III - Living

We don't have a language for the senses. Feelings are images,
sensations are like musical sounds. —Anais Nin

15. Experiencing: *Your sensual and curious self*

Now you are ready to delve into your shadow as well as your light. It's time to experience and accept all the parts that are *you*.

We are taught from the earliest age to repress, smother, and crush our negativity. "Be nice." "Don't be selfish." "That's greedy."

But children are born eager and desirous and hungry for experience and worldly things. Everything is exciting to them. They don't mean to be selfish—they mean to honor their humanness!

How can you regain that long ago thrill you felt when you experienced something new and exciting? Whether discovering a new flower, a leaf, a stone, a pinecone, you were imbued with wonder and so much desire you even wanted to taste it! You may not remember, but chances are if you saw something that intrigued you when you were little, you put it in your mouth!

And... you were quickly reprimanded. *"No!" "That's dirty!" "Ick"*!

By now you're repressed, anxious, and nervous when there's something that you desire. You don't pour yourself into experience with the wholehearted abandon you felt as a child.

But experience is your friend—even your best friend. If you don't meet it, and have a friendly chat, it will haunt you with fears, fantasies, crushed longings, which can begin to run your life.

Experience evokes images, fantasies, longings, and desires that are crucial in this journey. If you don't delve into your shadow side in this process, you'll never be a whole, integrated, happy human being.

Here's the truth: As a human being, having an earthly substance, you experience Life through, primarily, your five senses. What fabulous faculties our senses are. Think of the sense of taste— how delectable, how glorious is a taste of fresh sweet lemon or the first sip of a tea.

But our senses are hardly used in the way they could be. We eat as best we can—often on the run. We hardly glance at the vistas around us—usually we're late for an appointment or for work. We drive the same commute daily, surrounded by cars and frustration. Our vision becomes impaired by our desire *not* to see. The same with sounds. If you live in a city, you have to shut out the screech of the subway or the ringing of sirens or you'll go crazy. Oftentimes, our lives become an exercise in dulling our senses, not in quickening them and bringing them to life.

In order to discover what you would do if there was nothing you had to do, get reacquainted with your sensory experience of life.

What brings you pleasure and joy? What do you loathe? What sends shivers down your spine?

If we are going to solve emotional problems, weight problems, environmental problems, or any problem, we have to understand the furnace inside that we are feeding. —Bernie Fallon, Goodology

Practice, Listen, and Improvise

Practice: *Develop your sensory experiences*

Start with your sense of taste. What would you eat and drink if it could be anything, any time? From the moment we were born, we were put on scheduled feedings, we were told what was good for us, many foods were limited or forbidden, liquor was either a poison or a Hollywood glamor nectar. No wonder many of us are confused about food.

The only thing you need to know about taste is that you love it, in the same way that it loves you. Taste loves to be tasted. As the Sufis said, a strawberry cannot taste itself. As a human being, this is uniquely *your* experience, not the strawberry's. And not only that, but you can appreciate the experience of taste, because you can think about it, imagine it, and feel it.

How do you get past all the food shoulds and diets and budgets and really get to the freedom of experiencing this fabulous sense of taste in all its glory?

Start with nothing. Clean out your kitchen shelves, your refrigerator, your freezer. Imagine your kitchen to be a plot of earth in early March where nothing is growing, but the seeds are getting all excited as the earth begins to warm deep underground.

What would you eat if you could eat anything at all?

Eat what you love. I don't care what it is—I don't care how fattening or sweet or salty or sour or bitter ... *love the taste.*

All that matters is that whatever you put in your mouth is made from the freshest, best ingredients it can be.

This is something my mother taught me, and you can read more about it in a cookbook she wrote called *Beyond Measure*. It doesn't matter what the recipe is, or what you mix together, just so long as all the ingredients are fresh and pure. Nowadays, we need to specify 'organic' and local and so forth, but not all that long ago we could eat a carrot from our neighbor's backyard without worrying about poisonous pesticides. We need to go back to that—including the fresh dirt that clings to the carrot. As much as possible, taste items that are local, fresh, organic.

Although you might binge in the beginning with the foods you crave, you'll find you're satisfied with less in the long run, *because your taste buds are satisfied.* Your taste buds need nourishment as much as your senses of sight and sound. Be kind to them.

Instead of hating food, or being annoyed that you have to cook a dinner for your family, or feeling the pressure of shopping, join a CSA and work with whatever happens to be available that week. It'll get your creative juices flowing. If there isn't a CSA near you, visit a local farmer's market. Enjoy the freshness, the sweetness, the unusual, the integrity.

If you eat meat, have integrity around that as well. It may be more expensive to purchase meat that's been raised and killed humanely, but I guarantee that not only will you feel healthier, it will *taste* better.

By going back to the source of what you love to eat, and eliminating all the guilt and pressure associated with food and cooking that permeates our culture (either you 'love' to cook or you 'hate' to cook—or you're good or you're bad at it ...) you can get to the essence of *what would you eat if you could eat or drink anything.*

Ice cream? Potato chips? Chocolate? Wine?

Get only the best. Make your own. If you're going to make your own ice-cream, use the best, farm-fresh milk you can find. The flavor will be different—more rich and delicious. If you want to use white, refined sugar, enjoy it. Look at the amazing whiteness twinkling in the sunshine. *Look* at it. Then dip your finger in it and taste. Savor. *Enjoy.*

Use sea salt. There are so many delicious salts to try! In England we used Maldon sea salt, which forms into the most delightful hexagonal crystals—some quite large, which we'd have to crumble into our food. The taste was *tasty*—not salty. Sure it's expensive, but you're not trying to make a dish more salty, instead you're using salt to enhance its flavors—so get the tastiest salt, not the saltiest.

If you love chocolate, buy the best. You'll eat less and you'll enjoy it more.

Make your own potato chips using local, organic potatoes. Commercial potatoes are some of the vegetables most heavily permeated with pesticides because the chemicals saturate the earth in which they're grown and imbue the potato from the time it's tiny. I found this out when I read *The Botany of Desire* by Michael Pollan.

I also learned this: In the Andes Mountains of Peru, potatoes were domesticated more than 8,000 years ago. More than 5,000 varieties of potatoes are still grown there today. But when the Spaniards took potatoes back to Europe a few centuries ago, the concept of crop variety and diversity was lost to the desire for control and profit. By growing only one kind of potato, biological pests were able to wipe out a nation's entire potato crop, as happened in Ireland.

In the United States, we still want to control the potato, using methods from fertilizers and pesticides to genetic engineering.

Pollan even quotes a commercial potato farmer who says that he, personally, only eats potatoes he grows himself in his own backyard.

So you can see how even something as seemingly lowly as a potato takes on a life of its own if you pay attention to it!

Listen: *Sound*

This practice needs to be done in nature. Even if you live in the heart of the city, you'll need to find a place that has some nature nearby, whether it's sitting on a bench under a scraggly dusty tree and hearing one pigeon coo or walking along the river so you can hear the water. A city near the sea will always have seagulls somewhere near. Or is there a small park nearby with a fountain?

We tend to listen for sounds we're attuned to—the voice of a friend, for example, or a song we enjoy hearing. This exercise in listening has to do with activating forces that are speaking to you in a different language—and come from a different source than your friendly and responsive brain.

Take twenty minutes to listen to everything going on around you. If you're walking as you do this, focus exclusively on sound. That means keeping your eyes half-glazed, focused on a point on the horizon, without really paying attention to what you see. Let the vibration of sound penetrate you. If you can lie on the beach, listen to the waves, over and over—focusing only on that sound.

I'll always remember the time I went birding early one morning with a master birder called Kai Reed. Our group entered the forest and, following Kai, began our walk, binoculars around our necks, eagerly scanning the treetops.

Kai, however, gazed intently at the ground as he walked.

"What's he doing?" I asked, puzzled.

"Listening," someone replied.

And that's how he found his birds! Every so often he'd pause, lift his binoculars, and point out a Baltimore oriole or a duckwing sparrow. Then we'd proceed, and he'd be gazing down again—hardly seeing—at the ground.

Listening.

I followed his lead, and soon began hearing the sounds of birds I'd never heard before. The woods became filled with birdsong. The more I did this, the more I was able to distinguish one bird call from another.

In just a single morning, I had activated my consciousness of sound to a dramatic degree.

What sounds would you listen to if you could choose? Do the ocean waves speak to you, or the heart of the sounds of a forest at dusk, or the songbirds at dawn?

The reason I don't include music in this exercise is that music uses a different part of your processing system. It stimulates memories, nostalgia, sentimentality, other people ... but it doesn't typically bring you to the same core stillness that active listening in nature brings. You want your ears to be seeking and meditating on vibrations that aren't filtered through machines. We are vibrations and you need to tune into yours.

Another exercise is this one: Before you go to sleep, lie in the dark and listen to the sounds that are closest to you. Usually this is the sound of your own breathing. That is the sound nearest and dearest to our heart.

Now listen to the sound that is just a bit farther away—perhaps the sound of breathing from a friend or a pet. Listen actively to the sound.

Now move your sense of sound to the outer fringes of the room—the creak of the house if it's windy outside, for example. The rain pattering on the roof. If you live in an apartment building, try to hear through walls. Don't strain, but focus your attention.

Now focus on the street or garden outside your house. Move your consciousness around your building and listen. A car goes by. An owl hoots. The rustle of leaves in the tree.

Now imagine you're hearing even farther away from where you're lying in the dark. When I lived in Greenwich Village I could start hearing cars all the way on 6th Avenue and if there was the rumble of a truck I could hear it for a long, long time if I concentrated hard enough. If you're in the country, let your consciousness flow outward into the woods or mountains, listening very hard for the sounds that penetrate the night. It's never as quiet as you might imagine. Go out further and further, till you encompass your town or city, your state, and you even hear sounds from distant places in the country—the desert or the ocean... by this time you may have fallen asleep, and that's fine too. Your sense of sound has been activated to a profound degree.

You can do this exercise if you tend to wake up in the middle of the night—it's one of the best cures for insomnia I've ever come across.

Improvise: *Desire*

Okay, now here's one more to consider: your relationship with sex and the life-affirming experience of sexual desire.

How have you come to be who you are sexually? How do you cope with the forces of attraction and desire? How do you perceive the difference between love and eroticism? Or between a mystical connection and a physical one?

I am not a sex therapist and do not claim to have answers or solutions. I think each one of us has to discover and experience our own insight into our personal desires.

But I do know this: your desires are as crucial in this journey as are your longings. Follow them—feel them—honor them.

Desire is a delicious compass that guides you toward your star.

Be brave enough to do some exploration on your own regarding your personal desires. Sift through the hang-ups, longings, frustrations, and expectations that have crushed this part of you from the very beginning when you first heard the word "no."

Explore the dichotomy between love and desire and how this has played out in your life. Discover how your ideal of pleasure has evolved from when you were a child to where you are now.

Your task during this stage of your journey is to know and understand the nature of desire, and how it plays into your life now. Once you understand it, you can more fully appreciate and integrate it into the life you want to create for yourself in the future.

Those who restrain desire, do so because theirs is weak enough to be restrained.
—William Blake

What is born will die,
What has been gathered will be dispersed,
What has been accumulated will be exhausted,
What has been built up will collapse,
And what has been high will be brought low.
—Sogyal Rinpoche

16. Leaving behind: *Everything that no longer serves you*

At various times in our lives we inevitably encounter unexpected losses, earth-shattering events, a surprising shift, an end of an era. When values, beliefs, relationships, situations or other aspects of our lives become outmoded they must be left behind or there is no room for fresh growth.

The experience can be a deeply wounding, traumatic event.

At the same time, or perhaps later, it can be an enormous relief.

The end of an era is something that is not typically a choice we make. It's not like natural death, which is organic—it's more like a bolt of lightning that shatters your world. It happens to you, rather than you growing into it.

When you come to the end, there is no going back. What you had cannot be rebuilt. Something fresh and entirely new has to take its place.

This experience can be devastating—the loss of a spouse, or a house, or a job. It's always some sort of loss.

And yet, an era does not end until you are ready, no matter how unready you may feel. There are inevitably times in your life when you have to give up, move on, leave something or someone behind, embrace something new.

There are all sorts of people in the world. What sort are you? Some people enjoy being busy, for example. They wake up in the morning with energy and optimism, ready to tackle the task at hand. Without a project or place to go, they feel lost and perhaps a bit anxious.

Other people may long to leave the duties of what feels like a daily grind behind and go on a long voyage, or paint a picture, or, at the very least, take a nap!

Which person are you? If you haven't tried a different lifestyle, how do you know for sure? Do you feel you *should* be busy and work hard, or do you enjoy it? Does hanging out with friends give you a deep sense of satisfaction and pleasure, or do you feel slightly bored and wish there was different you could be doing?

The practice of elimination will help you to distinguish between what is essential and what is not any longer. Everyone is different, and no one but you knows who you really are. You need to assess what is no longer necessary as you move forward and what it is *you* want to sustain, to keep, and to renew.

Have nothing in your houses that you do not know to be useful, or believe to be beautiful. —William Morris

Practice, Listen, and Improvise

Practice: *Clear your space*

By practicing the elimination of everything that you don't need any more, whether or not you realize that you don't, you are opening yourself to a new way of looking at your life.

Practice letting go of everything that no longer serves you. Eliminate everything that you don't love, or need, or find beautiful.

Start with a closet—clear it out. If there's something in there that you haven't used or worn for a year, pass it along to someone who will use it. If there's something in there that you absolutely have to keep (IRS papers, for example) put them somewhere safe, but not in a closet that you use on a day-to-day basis.

Throw out old toiletries, outdated spices from your kitchen cupboard, and clean out your refrigerator. Scour your shelves for books that you haven't read, won't read, don't need. By passing these things along to someone who will read them, you're energizing a tremendous flow in your life and in the universe.

Start with one room at a time. This process can take as long as you need it to. A library full of books may take a few months to cull. Some people like to choose one book a day to give away; others do it all at once.

Your wardrobe—especially if you get some help—may take only a few hours. Or it may take weeks. Ask for help from a friend if you get stuck.

Be ruthless—you won't regret getting rid of the weight of everything that is no longer essential to you. Use this adage as you sort: *"When in doubt, throw it out."* If you're not sure whether or not you want to keep that shirt, out it goes. Only keep that which you love—what really matters to you. Or what is absolutely essential to your well-being.

Emptiness offers the space and time for you to look around and experience peace in your immediate environment.

Clear the clutter from your physical space and sit with the emptiness for a while. Eventually you'll begin to get a sense for what you want to grow in that emptiness.

Listen: *Clear your schedule*

Now that you've cleared your physical space, clear your daily schedule. Stop doing anything that no longer serves you.

How can you tell? Most of the time, if an appointment makes you feel stressed, chances are you can let it go. Cancel appointments, business meetings, social engagements, or errands unless they are essential.

Having your teeth cleaned at the dentist may make you feel stressed, but in the long run you'll be glad you kept that appointment. An obligation to go out to a movie when you'd rather stay home is less essential. Assess what is important.

If you have a responsibility that is stressful but also brings you joy, that's important. For instance, say you are a musician. The details and complications of preparing for a concert may feel overwhelming but the joy of performing ultimately makes it worthwhile.

The same holds true if you are responsible for a young child. Your passion and commitment to your child is stronger than the stress that accompanies the work involved. Just because an activity is hard or challenging does not mean it is not vital.

Be gentle with yourself when you make the list. Weigh the importance of your many obligations. When in doubt, simplify your daily schedule as much as possible, even if you are afraid you might be bored. Remove everything from it that no longer serves you. Make a list of appointments, responsibilities, pleasures, issues—everything that gives you a vaguely uneasy feeling in the pit of your stomach.

Ask yourself, "Is it vital that I do that?"

Keep the appointments, responsibilities, and duties that bring you joy or those without which you would not be able to experience joy in some other way.

Improvise: *Clear your beliefs*

Explore your beliefs about yourself and your life and your world.

Roles: Get a piece of paper, cut it into small pieces, and write down all the roles that you've played throughout your life. Examples are 'son', 'sister', 'housekeeper', 'CEO', 'good student', 'dreamer.' Now burn each of these in a ritualistic little ceremony.

Shoulds: Get another piece of paper and write down all the "shoulds" in your life. 'Always have dinner ready at six.' 'Call my aunt every Friday.' 'Be better at bookkeeping.' 'Be more creative.' 'Cut my hair.'

Your 'shoulds' may take some soul-searching to discover, because they are often so deeply ingrained in our lives that often we don't notice them anymore. You might find this task easier to accomplish over the course of a week or a month. Every day think about one 'should' in your life and write it down on a small piece of paper.

Then burn it—set it alight in your sink and wash the ashes down the drain.

Beliefs: Get another piece of paper, cut it into smallish pieces, and write down your beliefs. All of them that you can think of—

even those you want to hold onto. If they are necessary as part of the new you who emerges at the end of this journey, they will still be there, but cleansed, fresh, and stronger.

These can range from "I do/don't believe in God," to a superstition, to a belief in yourself (negative or positive).

In the case of examining and releasing a belief, it may not be that you don't need it any longer or that it no longer holds true for you. But you still need to sift out beliefs that have settled into a dusty corner of your semi-consciousness, and now are cluttering your path to create your life the way you want it, from your beliefs that empower you to move forward.

Burn them all. The beliefs that continue to hold true for you will do so no matter what, and those that are dead weight will be released.

Now: Imagine looking at a bare plot of earth in the early spring and wondering what to plant there.

You only lose what you cling to. –Buddha

⚊

Each of us has a star that prefers us above all others. This is the star of our imagination that follows us for ourselves alone. It is that most mysterious star of our individuality telling us we make a difference.
—Jane Eliot, Beyond Measure

17. Friendship: *Who matters?*

You've released everything in your life that no longer serves you.

The question now is not what remains, but *who* remains.

Friends are the most sacred part of your life, and friendships the most valuable. Often we take friends for granted, or hold onto friends from the past simply because we feel obligated or out of a sense of shared nostalgia. Or we enjoy meeting new people, and intensely conversing with them, and yet the relationship remains superficial.

If you pause to think about it, though, friends create a circle around you unlike anything else. They are *chosen* by you.

Not only that, but psychological studies have shown that good friends are the best antidotes to illness, depression, and even aging and death.

Friendships may have a far more powerful impact on our well-being than even family members do.

Who are your friends? This next stage has to do with the people who surround you in your daily life.

Who are they?

> *Friendship with oneself is all-important because without it one cannot be friends with anyone else in the world.* —Eleanor Roosevelt

Practice, Listen, and Improvise

Practice: *Surround yourself*

Draw a large bubble on a fresh page, and inside write the name of a current friend.

Using a different color, draw another bubble within that one and write a few words describing what this person is like—not in relationship to you, but in relationship to themselves. Are they successful, struggling, devoted, angry....

Now draw a second circle within the large circle and write down an equally objective description of how you see yourself, not in relation to your friend, but in relation to you and your own life. Use a similar style of describing yourself, even if your lifestyle is very different. Be as objective as you can.

The third circle you're going to draw overlaps both those smaller circles and describes *your* role in the relationship. Are you caretaker, golfing buddy, sister, confidante, lover? Write down as many words as you can to describe yourself in this relationship.

A fourth bubble is the "value" bubble. In this bubble write down all the aspects of the friendship you value.

The fifth and last bubble is the "release" bubble. In here write down all the aspects of the friendship that are exhausting, debilitating, negative.

On a fresh page, create a new large bubble and write the name of a different person. Repeat this exercise with all your friends.

Listen

Look at the bubbles you've created and examine them as though they are alive. Really take into your heart whether or not these friends are nourishing, enjoyable, positive, supportive people you want to surround yourself with.

If they are, honor them. Be even more creative in your encounters. Do something together that's different. Be spontaneous. Have fun.

If they aren't, then gently let them go. You don't have to make a big deal about this—but you can be busy when they call, or be slow about returning calls.

One thing I have learned over the years is that you (and they!) may think you are hurting their feelings by pulling away, but often your impact on them is just as draining as theirs is on you. Sometimes friendships really do need to take a break, at the very least, or released, if necessary. Trust that you know when.

Many of us have friends whom we have known since preschool, before we fell in love or moved to a different country. Sometimes they precede marriage and family, and many are still around even if a spouse dies or we get divorced, or after your children have left home.

If you were dying, who would you want to be beside you? Imagine that same urgency, terror, and awe in your daily life and ask yourself the same question. *Who would I like to have nearby?*

Improvise: *Make something up*

Friends are there, ideally, to give you hope. They encourage, support, critique, and enjoy you for you who are.

Here's something random to do: Invent something new together. Something practical, beautiful, silly, useful, or fun. Or all of those things!

Do it with a friend.

> *The bird a nest,*
> *the spider a web,*
> *man friendship.*

—William Blake

Night, the beloved. Night, when words fade and things come alive. When the destructive analysis of day is done, and all that is truly important becomes whole and sound again. When man reassembles his fragmentary self and grows with the calm of a tree. —Antoine de Saint-Exupery, Flight to Arras

18. Dreaming: *Mysteries of the unconscious*

You are not alone. But your best friend through the journey may not be the person you think.

It is your unconscious.

Your unconscious knows you better than you know yourself.

Your unconscious is the interpreter between your conscious will activity and your Spirit self.

It is your healer. Your enlightener.

Where do you meet? *In your dreams.*

Through sleep and dreams, you can access this deep, creative self-knowledge and self-understanding. You can journey outside your body, travel outside the supposed limitations of time and space, encounter spiritual guides in other dimensions.

If you practice lucid or conscious dreaming, it can also become one of the greatest adventures of your life.

Lucid or conscious dreaming is the ability to be self-aware while you're asleep and dreaming. Eventually, you'll not only be aware that you're dreaming, but you'll actually be able to guide and create your dreams.

Remembering your dreams is just the beginning of an exploration unlike any other. Often you'll find that just by remembering a dream you'll experience a feeling or insight that filters into your day.

But imagine being able to create that feeling or insight yourself! Imagine being able to observe, sense, hear, smell as vividly as you can when you are awake and conscious!

A lucid dream is a co-created experience. What you're doing is interacting with your subconscious mind and imaging worlds and experiences into existence.

You can be inspired as an artist.

You can discover the source of an illness and heal yourself.

You can control nightmares or terrors that have been troubling you.

You can solve a problem.

You can fulfill wishes.

You can act on your desires.

You can ask questions and you can hear answers.

For example, you can consciously ask "Is it beneficial for me to move to Florida?" and your subconscious self will respond.

Or you can ask about a person or a job or the past or the future!

You can go on the greatest adventure of all: the exploration of your inner self.

There is a great deal of research on the effects of lucid dreaming, and I urge you to plunge in as deeply as you feel compelled to. I dreamed consciously when I was a child, but was not aware of what I was doing until a friend gave me a copy of Robert Moss's *Conscious Dreaming* when I was as adult. Then I discovered that what I'd been doing for years actually had a name. Robert Moss's own experience of childhood dreams was so similar to my own I felt I'd met a kindred spirit.

Immediately I launched into the practice of creating my conscious dream experiences, rather than believing the experience to be random and hoping they would happen on their own.

There's plenty of information out there on the hows, whys, and wherefores of conscious dreaming. Scientists have done enough experiments by now to demonstrate that it enables you to remember an instruction from when you were conscious and then to act on it while you're dreaming. It also is known to produce a highly active brainwave frequency not associated with regular dreaming or even normal waking awareness.

Here I offer practices to start you off on the adventure of a lifetime.

> Hen'elele ka moe na ke kanaka (A dream is a bearer of messages to man)
> —Hawaiian Proverb

Practice, Listen, and Improvise

Practice: *Remember your dreams.*

Even if you typically tell people "I never remember my dreams" you'll begin to remember now.

How? First of all, acknowledge the feeling you have when you wake from a dream, even if you don't remember the dream itself. Stay in the same position and let yourself become conscious of that feeling. Let it permeate you. Then remember just a tiny event that created that feeling. As days pass and you consciously pay attention to your feeling and perhaps the last image in your mind before you awoke, you'll recall the image before that last one.

If you do this regularly, recalling your dreams backward, you'll find that remembering your dreams becomes increasingly habitual.

Also, before you fall asleep at night, instruct your mind: *I want to remember my dreams when I wake up.*

Write down your dreams. Keep a dream journal by your bed, and before your eyes are fully open reach for your pen and begin to write. When you first begin a dream journal you may find you only have a few phrases or a small detail to write down. Your first associations are as important as the dream itself—write those down as well. The longer you keep it up, the more lengthy and vivid you'll find your entries become. If you wake up in the night, write down your dream as well, because chances are you won't remember it otherwise. Record your feelings as well as any images.

Read through your dream journal before you go to sleep. This will remind you as you're dreaming that you have a purpose: to remember and write down your dream.

State your intention. As you fall asleep, instruct your mind to lucid dream.

Meditate before sleeping. One thing I do is a relaxation technique of beginning with my toes and becoming conscious of each part of my body, including my organs and fingertips, and filling each part with light. Then I wrap my body in a rainbow cloak, and as I drift off to sleep, I feel assured that my physical body is safe and taken care of as I journey into far-off places.

Another powerful before-going-to-sleep exercise is to recall your day backward, all the way to the moment just before you woke up. Do this in a gliding motion, not dwelling on anything in particular or being anxious about trying to remember. Soar through the events and the people you met as though you were a great bird soaring through the experiences but not landing on any of them.

By meditating like this while you are falling asleep, you'll experience out-of-body projections, memories, auditory impressions, and intense revelations. And you'll increase your self-awareness in your dreams.

Get plenty of sleep. Be rested. Did you know that we dream all through the night—about one dream period every 90 minutes? As you get into the habit of lucid dreaming, you'll need plenty of time to wake up and record your dreams.

Listen: *Reality check*

While you are dreaming, pause to ask yourself "Is this real?" Look around and touch something. Try to smell or hear. Ask yourself "Who am I?" "Where did I come from?" This is key to becoming a conscious dreamer.

Become even more self-aware as you dream.

Where are you in your dream? Grow aware of location, especially if it repeats itself. Ask the question of someone you meet: Why here?

Who are you in your dream? Active or passive? Chatty or quiet? Notice.

After a while you will find that you can actually create the dream you want to have. This is sometimes called "incubating" a lucid dream. You can do it by stating your intention about the dream, or visualizing it frequently during the day.

Improvise: *There's the moon!*

Take a moon bath. As you lie in an open field under the full moon, or in a hammock on the roof of your building, let your own self-nurturing energy mingle with the moon's. The moon is mother, nurturer, unconsciousness, myth, and mystery.

Become aware of the moonsphere—the lunar influence that extends far beyond the light of the moon itself, into your subconscious and unconscious. Its sphere of action or influence is in everything liquid on earth, including much of your human body.

Purchase a calendar showing the moon phases and become aware of the phases of the moon in your daily life. If there's a project that you want to get started on, begin it as close as possible to the new moon. If you're planning an intervention for a friend, avoid scheduling it on a full moon when emotions are running very high.

Pay attention to the phases of the moon... you may find that heightening your relationship with the moon affects your dream life more than you imagine.

> *The night is forever. I can't sleep.*
> *The clear moon is so bright, so bright.*
> *I almost think I hear a voice call me,*
> *and to the empty sky say, Yes?*

> —Zi Ye

*Since money is intimately connected with human social life
and is a human invention not found in nature, is it possible that
money is also in a process of development?* –Siegfried E. Finser

19. Illuminating: *Seeing what is really there*

Sometimes it can be difficult to see things as they really are.
We all wear lenses that cause us to perceive a situation
from our individual point of view.

How can we learn to see things as they really are—without our
perception being fogged by anxiety, prejudice, doctrine,
misunderstanding, inner blindness?

Remember the story told by Buddha about the blind men and
the elephant? In the tale, a king was trying to put an end to the
ceaseless waste-of-time arguments that were occurring between
various sects regarding the definition of truth, and he

commanded all subjects who had been blind since birth to come to his palace. Then, the king asked for an elephant.

Some of the blind people were allowed to feel the head of the elephant, others were introduced to the ear, others to the tusk, the trunk, the body, the foot, the tail, and so on, to the tuft at the end of the tail. Each time the king allowed them to touch a part of the elephant, he said, "This, blind people, is what an elephant is like."

Afterward he asked them what the elephant was like. Some said like a water jar, others like a winnowing basket, others like an iron rod, others like the pole of a plow.

Still others described the elephant as a granary, a post, mortar, a pestle, and those who had felt the tuft at the end of the tail described the elephant as being just like a broom.

The blind men began arguing vehemently, and were soon brawling with each other, each group claiming that they were right and the others were wrong.

The moral of the story is self-evident.

And so now, with that story in mind, it's time to shed light on one of our most common and most misunderstood motivations: Money. Many of you will say, *I can't do whatever I want; I need to make money.* But if you've come this far toward finding your heart's desire, then you are ready for a deeper understanding of the nature of money and its potential impediment or gift in your daily life.

Talking about money is like blind men arguing about what an elephant looks like. There's an overwhelming amount of it and yet there never seems to be enough. It can be counted, but it's out of our control. It supports art and culture, yet it has nothing to do with the actual creating of art. It creates possibilities—and destroys them. The love of it is the source of evil. And it enables extraordinary, generous goodness. It enriches and ennobles. It creates greed and meanness.

Or does it seem to you equal to a pair of shoes or a quid pro quo?

Or do you want to stuff bills in the mattress, know they're there, and never let them go?

None of those things can totally sum up the concept of *money*. They are each, like a blind person feeling one part of an elephant, only one small aspect of money. *Your* aspect, *your* experience of money. Of course money is only worth as much as it can purchase, and another extreme view is that it is only useless bits of paper that make you feel secure. And of course money needs to flow and grow—money begets money in a capital world. Yes, money is the stuff dreams are made of, and if you let it, it can be a destroyer of dreams.

If we elevate money to the world of ideals, if we regard it as a tool to guide us to be free and helpful and generous, that's another form of money. If it becomes like a dead albatross that has no life of its own to share and generate and create relationships—in essence letting us be free to create our lives— then it can be deadly.

Be careful that your concept of money doesn't become a prison. It's very easy to let that happen. You need to make it, love it, give it, use it, enjoy it and if you don't have enough do not despair: Once you've got the basic necessities of life covered, you'll always have enough for what you need. The paradox is this: The less you have, the less you need.

If you use money to love and give and enjoy, you know this to be true. When you live in a world of generosity and goodness, good things happen, your financial world is activated, and things take place that otherwise would have been unavailable to you.

Work is love made visible. And if you cannot work with love but only with distaste, it is better that you should leave your work and sit at the gate of the temple and take alms of those who work with joy. –Khalil Gibran

Practice, Listen, and Improvise

Practice: *Take a good look at money*

Be like the sun. The sun sheds light on everything that's happening, equally. There's no judgment, no argument, no hidden secrets, no moodiness attached to the sun. It shows you what needs to be done, whether it's shining light on the cobwebs you haven't swept away or the roses that need tending. It clarifies, illuminates, and exposes. *It shows you what is really there.*

Take out your journal and describe, completely neutrally, without any emotion, your financial situation. Use number-symbols as much as possible, because they are inherently neutral. This does not have to be in list form. Draw the numbers and words in a circle or a map. Be creative. Call it "Finances— Illuminated."

Now, turn the page and describe your work situation. Exclude your financial compensation: just describe your duties, your hours, your coworkers. Describe all these as neutrally as you can. This is "Work—Illuminated." Write from the bottom of the page up, or in a spiral or circle. Or make a map of different areas of your work. Or, if you have more than one job or work-related activity, draw a map with different continents on it.

Perhaps you are currently unemployed, or you work at home, or you don't "have to" work. You still need to do this exercise.

Because this is the truth: no matter who you are, how rich or how poor—whether you're unemployed, or even a child, all human beings have a spiritual need to work. Even if you believe there is nothing you have to do, you still work. And if you don't, *you need to.*

This innate human need to work is wired in our brains. It's why millionaires are philanthropists and socialites volunteer. We teach our children to be responsible for chores before they earn money for them because certain things simply need to be done.

We watch our teenagers wrestle with their longing to be income-independent and yet entitled to that which they've always had.

We all work. We work to keep our house functioning and clean, we work at relationships, and we work at our hobbies.

The problem in our culture is that we have equated work with something that impedes our personal freedom and leisure. But just because we enjoy something that doesn't mean it's not work.

So what can you do?

Examine your two "lists." Take out your Finances Illuminated list and write down everything you would buy, share, invest—everything you would do if you had unlimited funds.

Now write another list of everything in your life that is non-essential. If you were stripped of everything you had, what would you do? What could you afford to lose? Work on this for a while. If you can do this exercise in a safe workshop group, you may be amazed at how much you discover you can let go of. You may find yourself imagining worse and worse scenarios, stripping away all the materialism of your life, piece by piece, until only what is essential remains with you. Perhaps it is a guitar, or a car, or your books.

See what you value most of all. This is a tremendous exercise, because you see really how little you need to exist.

You see really that, whether or not you are a trust fund baby or a barista or unemployed: it's not about the money, it's about the work.

Now, you have two choices.

The first is that you can work at a job that doesn't nourish your soul, but is fairly decent: you're working with good people, for a good cause or in a positive environment, and the paycheck covers the necessary bills.

If you have work like this, you'll need to experience your "what you would do if there was nothing you had to do" time in your after-hours. If you're an early riser, make dawn the time of sacred nothingness—and let what you really love doing emerge of its own accord. You may find you want to set up an easel and paint for an hour. Or take a long walk. Allow your passion to surface in spite of the hours you need to give to your other work.

If you have work that is what you'd choose to do, even if you didn't have to, your task is to honor that. Even people who say they love their work—the cut, thrust, and parry of a lawyer in the courtroom, a healing doctor meeting with patients all day, a musician practicing with his chamber group—tend to lose themselves and forget that what they're doing is not only for their paycheck, but because they enjoy it.

Most of us are somewhere in the middle. Work is bound to be stressful, to have its ups and downs. You *will* experience conflict with co-workers and challenging tasks. But these are *good* things! Seen through a positive lens, a day-long tussle with students and colleagues at an inner-city school may seem exhausting, but deep inside you, if it's the right work for you, you are exhilarated.

The point is that work is essential to our human existence. We are made to work. We love work. We actually love our duty. If children were shown how much we grownups love our work, and if we let them imitate us in playful pretending to work rather than so early making chores appear as drudgery, children would grow up already knowing the truth: that if there was nothing you had to do, *you'd still work.* You'd want to *do* something: whether it is volunteering at the library or at an animal rescue center or helping someone with homework or picking flowers to put in a vase.

If you tell me you are tied to a job you hate, if you are tired and exhausted, if you hate your boss, and you can't stand the work itself—then you need to quit. It's that simple. It may take months or years before you can figure out a way, but that is what you need to do. You *are* free to quit.

If you think you can't quit because of money constraints, then take your hour of nothing time to imagine what you would do in an ideal world. This one's hard if you've had a job you don't like for many years. But let your imagination soar. Practice seeing things as they really are.

You don't need to suffer a job that is soul-destroying.

One client of mine swore he hated all work, hated having to make money, and nothing to do with money could be satisfying or nourishing. After working through intense issues around money, I learned that he loved music and had been a record collector—even buying and selling used records when he was younger. He had never made enough money from it, and he loved his records, so he hated parting with them. Then I found out that he used to write his own songs and record them. We listened to a few recordings and I realized that because he did not think they were good enough to make money, he had dismissed something he loved doing. If he didn't have to go down into the coal mines (metaphorically speaking) every day, he admitted, he'd probably be puttering around with recording equipment and writing songs. He'd be collating his music library and connecting with other music lovers on the Internet.

It wasn't long before he realized that he could do that anyway. He felt he might lose his love for music if he had to make money at it, so I didn't urge him to find a paying job in the field he loves (although that might come later, after he realizes money is not an evil force that destroys everything in your path—it's actually a cheerful, good-natured friend that you'd like to have around all the time!). Instead, I urged him to schedule at least one hour a day and more on weekends to devote to his real 'work'—even if he considers it a hobby.

What it comes down to, ultimately, is balance. Parents of young children rarely allow themselves this balance. When a toddler lies down to nap, most of the time the parents are running around trying to catch up on phone calls and laundry—things they feel they can't do when their child is awake. This goes back to our experience of time. There's actually plenty of time to do whatever it is you want to do. If you give yourself enough time to get from hither to thither, you find you don't have to rush, right?

So it is with life: give yourself the time to rest, to play, to do something you love doing, to be still and love yourself—and you'll find there's always time for that. You just have to schedule it.

The other day someone moaned about the fact that her yoga class was so early and she hated that. She had to be there at six and apparently her teacher is mean and tough, and if she doesn't show up regularly she'll kick her out of the class.

Well, that doesn't sound very yoga-like to me, and six a.m. seems awfully early for someone who isn't typically awake then. She replied, "It's the only time I can go to yoga. I'm flat out with work for the rest of the day and social events in the evening. Every hour is booked solid."

I started to remind her that she could just as easily book a yoga class into the middle of the day as she could book a client. Who has declared this work week of 40 or, in her case, 60+ hours to be essential to success and health? And recent studies have proven that after forty hours of work, productivity diminishes anyway.

But my friend felt absolutely that she couldn't possibly change her lifestyle to make room for a noon or afternoon yoga class, so I let it go.

It amazes me how most of the working world feels constrained by a vague entity or force that has created rules we follow without giving any thought to the idea that there are other ways of experiencing the day and that, more often than not, we are able to make our own rules.

Listen: *Look at yourself and your situation without glasses*

When Dorothy, the Scarecrow, the Tin Woodman, and the Cowardly Lion entered the glorious Emerald City they were given special protective glasses to shield their eyes from the mystical green brilliance.

Only when they took their glasses off and saw that the Emerald City was just an ordinary city, that it was the glasses they wore that made it glow and sparkle and gleam in that awesome emerald light, were they able to see things as they were.

Take off your glasses, look at these many maps you've created, and study them. See how you can develop them further.

Try to get to the root of your view of work and money.

If your work is something you love so much you'd be doing it even if you were a billionaire—whether you're a gardener or accountant or inventor—then imagine it in a different way. Imagine doing it artistically rather than to make money or to grow your business.

If your great passion is counting money—or watching your investments—try to look at that activity artistically as well. What happens to money that is creative and productive? Investigate good things that can happen from the money you make.

What makes you feel good about money? Is it security? Is it freedom? Is it beauty? Look at all the positive aspects of money, and imagine how you could best put your wealth into your highest goals and imaginings. Become conscious of its goodness and why you love it and it loves you.

Improvise: *Be creative with finances*

Think outside the money-box.

Do something with money that you have never done before. If you have a rigid habit with everything you make (say each week you divide your paycheck between bills, savings, leisure, and charity), then mix it up a little.

Be poetic with money. Imagine it as a something alive and friendly. My local co-op market has a new alternative for payment: I deposit money into my account there. My co-op card has the balance on it, and what I owe for groceries is deducted from my account when I make a purchase. No cash, no checks, no credit or debit card, no banks necessary. I think that's a forward-thinking way to manage money.

When my son graduated from high school and was planning to major in economics at college, I invested, as a gift in his name, a small amount in RSF Social Finance. RSF, instead of making a huge profit for its stockholders, invests your money in innovative social enterprises in three areas: food and agriculture, education and the arts, and ecological stewardship. My son gets a monthly newsletter that includes articles about what "work" his money is doing in the world, for the good of the world.

RSF Social Finance is not the only business that is imagining money in an entirely new way. Here are some other businesses to explore:

- Certified B Corporation
- Green America
- Greenmont Capital Partners
- Imprint Capital Advisors
- New Resource Bank
- Pacific Community-Ventures
- Renewal2 Investment Fund
- Roots of Change
- Slow Money
- Social Ventures Network
- TBL Capital

Some companies want to change the phrase we've heard for most of lives from "venture capital" to "nurture capital."

And from "making a killing" to "making a living."

Have you heard about the Slow Money movement? "You don't have to think of yourself as an investor or be a revolutionary to join Slow Money. You just have to believe that millions of small financial acts—small donations, small investments, small acts of bringing money back down to earth—can add up to big change.

Change in our local food systems. Change in our national food system. Change in our economy."

Let your imagination soar.

What if companies gave away 50 percent of their profits?

What if we as consumers agreed to pay for what an item is really worth, including all of its environmental impacts and disposal costs, rather than trying to get something that's cheaply made, with cheap labor that exploits our fellow humans?

What if...

Start imagining our money-world in a different way.

There are hundreds, perhaps thousands, of ways to look at money in a new light.

Now get involved in a way that resonates with *you*.

*I just happen to think that in life we need to be a little like the
farmer who puts back into the soil what he takes out.* —Paul Newman

Each one of us has it in themselves to be a free spirit, just as every rose bud has in it a rose. –Rudolf Steiner

20. Consciousness: *What it means to be free*

In essence we live in a world made up of

- inorganic matter
- organic or alive matter, and
- consciousness of our existence.

It always amuses me when scientists try to "prove" the existence of spirit using methods that can really only be used to assess inorganic matter. The objects under consideration may have characteristics such as mass or charge, but the external arrangement of the objects, their relative motion, collision, and so forth, determine everything. The purpose of scientific investigation in physics, for instance, is to arrange and experiment with the external factors so that an occurrence is so-called "proven."

Likewise, in researching organic material, scientists need to take into consideration that the organic world is always changing. That's the meaning of being alive. But what is the living principle that operates and animates within the organic forms? Try as we might, we have still not discovered the "secret" of life. We still cannot bring an inanimate object to life. A chair remains a chair, no matter how many chemicals we coat it with or spells we cast.

What differentiates "life" from dead matter and why do we suppose we can use the same methods of understanding them? We need a much more intuitive way to understand it. Even researching genetics or agriculture needs to be approached not so much by how the environment impacts the object (as in inanimate events) but how the object affects the environment as well. These are two very different approaches.

The third approach is *your own personal relationship* to and experience with inanimate objects and life forces.

When your thinking engages with the world of experience, *you become conscious*. Unlike outer scientific experiment, this moment of consciousness opens inside you a vast world of insight.

You are capable of self-observation. *You are capable of consciousness.*

Not only does your mind think, but it *observes* itself thinking!

Not only that, but you can make up your thoughts, and you are *conscious* of what you create in your thinking.

Instead of believing yourself stuck in a world of organic and inorganic matter that already exists, you are able to create a world that completes the organic and inorganic world in which you live. You create what Rudolf Steiner calls a "world-process" that is uniquely your own.

Friend, you are not a passive onlooker of environment, genetics, and evolution. You are an active co-creator of your own world-process. This can happen when your *experience* encounters your *thinking*, for in that moment of meeting, your consciousness of that moment sets you free to create your life.

In that moment, you truly *are* free.

> *"But you were always a good man of business, Jacob," faltered Scrooge, who now began to apply this to himself.*
> *"Business!' cried the Ghost, wringing its hands again. "Mankind was my business; charity, mercy, forbearance, and benevolence, were, all, my business. The deals of my trade were but a drop of water in the comprehensive ocean of my business!"*
>
> –Charles Dickens, A Christmas Carol

Practice, Listen, and Improvise

Practice: *Rebirth*

We are born over and over again, throughout our lives.

Working with this book you have gone through a process of eliminating everything that no longer serves you, and welcoming everything that nourishes, inspires, and illuminates you.

You've seen that rebirths can be experienced in a relationship, or your job, or within a community, without necessarily moving to a new place.

You may have chosen to move. Perhaps you feel that it is imperative that you begin anew without the constraints and judgments you have put on yourself from the past. Or you have decided to eliminate a toxic relationship or job.

As the Hindus say, everyone is different. *Choose your own way.*

I hope you have discovered that by developing your inner world—the one that cannot be affected by any outward circumstances or situations—you are free.

Here is a review of the essential keys you need to open your doors to co-creating your world process:

Reverence. The quality of devotion to life is, in a sense, the ground you walk on in this journey. Be grateful for anything and everything that comes your way. The practice here is to become super-conscious of any thought you have of disrespect, meanness (toward yourself and others), arrogance. Negativity paralyzes your growing self-awareness and the realization that you are free to co-create your world. Don't go there.

Reflection. Become conscious of the depth and wealth of your *inner* life. This is the tender, beautiful part of you that combines thought with feeling. The experience of reading a profound poem that moves you is an example of this. Try to bring that experience into your everyday life, with every experience. We tend to separate poetic beauty, or listening to a delightful song, or a wonderful walk in the woods from our everyday tasks and experiences. Change that. Experience every action inwardly, as well as outwardly.

Tranquility: Instead of feeling that a task is hopeless, know that *your* task is to do the best you can at the time.

Find some time each day to be by yourself to meditate. Meditation helps your soul learn to distinguish between the essential and the nonessential. If you're stressed, upset, nervous, or angry, this is the time to objectify those emotions and regard them with no judgment and no connection. Separate yourself from them, acknowledge them, and release them. You remain a calm island in the sea of experience and will find yourself immeasurably refreshed and strong.

Just doing this for ten minutes each day will help to create inside you the tranquility you need to discover the world you *want* to create for yourself.

You'll learn how to become your *own* guide.

Listen: *Enjoy!*

One of my father's friends while growing up was the poet Robert Lax. He stayed with us for a while when we lived in Greece and then he later moved to Patmos where he lived the rest of his life, writing some of the most remarkable poems ever written.

My dad tells this story: At one time when he was feeling very low, he visited Bob on Patmos and told him his troubles. They went for a long walk on the beach, while my father described his situation. He ended with the heartfelt question,

"What should I *do?*"

They walked on in silence, then finally Bob paused, looked up, and pronounced,

"You need to *enjoy!*"

Robert Lax understood something essential about your existence: *Your duty is to enjoy the world you are creating.*

It's much easier to be anxious or worried. It's ingrained in us, from the time we're small. We're told to "be careful" and "don't touch that" and we're warned over and over about the terrible things that might happen if...

But we were born to enjoy. Remember the experiences you had as a child that filled you with pleasure and delight? Write down as many as pop into your head: eating ice cream outside on the porch in the middle of the night when it was too hot to sleep. The swimming hole. The bicycle under the tree on Christmas morning. Blowing dandelion seeds into the wind. The first snowfall. Flying a kite.

As an exercise, write down several things that give you pleasure today. Noticing these things will increase the experience of joy exponentially. Be positive. If you don't like the snow because you typically associate it with scraping car windshields and shoveling and skidding off the road, change that. Notice each flake. Listen to the stillness, the quiet. Take a walk in it. Cozy up by a fire.

See how you can experience it differently, just by deciding to?

It doesn't negate the fact that you have to shovel the snow or scrape your windshield. But it does acknowledge the beauty and serenity of falling snow.

Over time, this exercise helps you to experience the ultimate joy you have *in being free.*

Improvise: *Serving others and the world*

Seek out a task that is in service to a project, a person, a cause. If you've discovered your passion, see how you can share it with people. If you are a jazz singer, become aware of how your singing brings joy to others. This way you will find far more fulfillment in your work than you would if you were only struggling to be successful for yourself. Imagine the joy you give to others, just by standing up on that stage and crooning from your heart.

Enjoyment is fundamental to this process, but it is worthless if you think that enjoyment is the goal.

It's not! It's a lovely aspect of it. But sharing, helping, caring, serving other human beings increases your own pleasure immeasurably. Each ripple of your activity widens, eventually encompassing an entire lake. You will feel the effect you have on others because of the increased joy you experience in yourself.

Yes, you need to find work that is ideal for you.

And then you need to engage in that work with others, help others, serve others, help the world, serve the world and its people.

Step outside of yourself, outside your own experience, and touch the fabric of the human experience as a whole. You are here to enrich and help and encourage other people, as well as yourself.

That is your work as a human being.

*I slept and I dreamed that life is all joy. I woke and I saw that life is all
service. I served and I saw that service is joy. –Khalil Gibran*

"As human beings, our greatness lies not so much in being able to remake the world—that is the myth of the 'atomic age'—as in being able to remake ourselves." –Gandhi

21. Being in the world: *Writing your story*

N ow let's get even more practical.

Essentially, you have discovered you are a being of light, of love, and of freedom. You have a notion—I hope—of your ideal.

Now you are ready to create the story of your life—the way you want it to be.

How?

Write the story you want to live.

Storifying our lives has been with us from time immemorial.

Psychologists have determined that we spend a great deal of time in fictional worlds, whether in daydreams, novels, conversation, advertisements, or life narratives. When all is tallied up, the decades we spend in the realm of fantasy outstrip the time we spend in the real world.

When you're reading a good story three things are happening inside you:

- You're curious

- You're predicting what might happen next

- You're emotionally engaged

The best learning tools are not facts and figures, bullet points, or text books. They are stories. Children remember stories far longer than dry facts. You'll learn from a story something that you can't really grasp any other way.

History of religion shows this to be true as well: stories are the essence of all religious doctrines. Doctrine is shrouded in myths and legends and peopled with tales and fables.

Making up stories can change the world, as books written about feminism, slavery, or children working in factories have shown.

We live through story. Advertisers know this—read a label on the back of a bottle of wine, for example, or think of the famous J. Peterman clothing catalogs. Story makes our lives *matter*.

If religions can do it, and countries can do it, and billion-dollar-advertising companies can do it, then you can do it too, as an individual.

Making up your own story can change *your* world.

You can create your own story. ***You can write the life you want to live.***

*We are not nouns, we are verbs. I am not a thing—an actor, a
writer—I am a person who does things—I write, I act—and I never know
what I'm going to do next. I think you can be imprisoned if you
think of yourself as a noun.* —Stephen Fry

Practice, Listen, and Improvise

Practice: *Write your story*

If you're having a hard time with how to write a story, here's a
step-by-step.

First, think of your story in five acts.

"Five acts" are a classic model for all Shakespeare plays, all
Hollywood movies, and all top-notch story-telling. You start with
the set-up, then head into action. Then there's an unexpected
event that sends you in another direction (conflict, trouble,
challenge)... then the climax—triumph over disaster! And finally
the epilogue. The place you want to be.

Simple, isn't it?

To begin with, outline your story in five paragraphs. You want
to get your whole story down on paper, so it's important not to
get lost in one or other of these "Acts."

Start by writing only one paragraph that describes the set-up.
Write it in the present tense. You can use first, second, or third
person—whatever inspires you. But be consistent.

This first paragraph takes you back to the beginning of this
book. *Start where you are.*

Describe your protagonist's (your) situation as it is now. Here's
an example:

"You wake up on Monday morning and you're still out of work.
The rest of the world is getting into cars, shoving their way into
subways, digging ditches, creating symphonies, and anticipating
fat paychecks. You're lying on a mattress (you sold your bed last
week) with no place to go, nothing to do, and a fat eviction

notice on your brown Formica kitchen counter. You were downsized a year ago from your job at the hospital, you've applied for 68 jobs since then, and now you've hit rock bottom."

You can add more detail, more background, as you wish, but you don't have to. Yet.

Now for the action. Remember, you're writing the story you want to live. Keep it light.

The phone rings. Or...

There's a loud noise down the street.

Or...

When you get to the third paragraph (which is the hardest part of this story-telling process) you'll need to assess the situation. Is this really what you wanted to have happen? What are the benefits and the pitfalls? How could you actually live a life so you're never in the situation again that you found yourself in at the beginning of the story?

Just being rehired for the same job won't get you out of the situation, because being fired will always hang over you as a possibility. You haven't changed your inward self in the process.

How can you do that?

How can you include a plot twist in your story that will move your story out of your longing to alleviate anxieties, terror, and stress and into a life that really doesn't require that?

How can you eliminate your preconceptions about what your life 'should' look like?

Be creative here. You can write as freely as you like.

Remember, this is only one story you'll be writing. There are others. And still others. You can write a mystery, a romance, or a travelogue.

Now on to the fourth paragraph: this is the climax, the "car chase." This is where you are chasing after everything you ever wanted. You are putting all the pieces in place that will get you there. There's a lot going on.

In your final paragraph, spend some time imagining and describing your ideal situation. Your ideal friends and lover. Where you are, and how, and what. Describe it beautifully, with feeling. Describe it morally, with goodness. Describe it truthfully, with authenticity.

Here are a few more tips to help you if you've never tried to write a short story before.

Be flexible. Just as in life, things happen as you write that you don't expect. Let yourself be surprised but not upset by an image or idea that emerges as you write. As you grow more flexible in your writing, and learn to trust it, you'll become more flexible in your life and able to bounce a bit when life hits you with unexpected curves.

Focus on the mind and heart of your protagonist (you). We tend to be far too conscious of what other people think of us or what society expects of us. This is your story, and your hero or heroine needs to be just that: a hero or heroine! In stories we admire someone who stands up to a critical neighbor or a harsh boss. In real life we tend to crumble.

Be someone you would admire.

Be brave. There's a bit of Chicken Little in all of us. The sky is always falling in some form or other! But take the pebble out of the feathers on your head and take courage.

Be positive. We are ridiculed for being positive from an early age. Cynicism is cooler. But being positive is a strengthening, enlightening, good thing to be.

A scene I'll never forget was written in Anne Tyler's novel *The Accidental Tourist*. Macon moans about his life and how awful people are. Muriel says how she took a job cleaning in the hospital so she could be near her husband as he lay dying. She says that she used to feel that way about people, but then she would look out the window that was high over the Emergency entrance and watch the ambulances driving up, and all these people would rush out of the hospital and surround it, and carry the injured or sick person inside and take care of them... and she realized people were wonderful.

Choose the characters for your story wisely. Begin by including people you know. Who do you want in your story? Who don't you want? What kinds of characters would be great to include in your story so when you read it years later you still enjoy it? You want to be with people who inspire you, not people who bring you down or who make you feel stuck.

Listen: *What do you love in your story?*

And now we come to the greatest part of writing your story:

Write about what you love.

What gives you the most pleasure? Imagine the ecstasy of being in love... and apply that feeling to something in your life that you would love to do.

Here is where you set your imagination free. Dare to dream. Imagine a life with absolutely no restrictions: *not one.*

Not money, not family, not health issues, nor your latest crush. If there weren't a boyfriend, a job, a child ... if everything was absolutely taken care of, what would you do right now, *today?*

I'll tell you something I found very interesting when I first started counseling people through this process: Everyone's ideal is different! I assumed we'd all be pretty much the same— whether it's sleeping all day, or wanting to go to Hawai'i .... But once you've used the keys I've given you here and opened each door with all your heart, you emerge with insights that are entirely your own.

It's possible that the love of your life was something you'd forgotten and buried many years ago.

Buy that watercolor set and go to the south of France and paint for the summer?

Lie on the couch for a week and see no one—do nothing?

Cook up a storm?

Have a party—with caterers and helpers—the works?

Hang out with your children—go on picnics or take them to a place you long to show them?

And you may think that what you would love to do is go on a cruise around the world, but once you really investigate it, the initial infatuation with the idea fades. You learn about the excess, the damage to the ocean, the boredom of being stuck with people you don't necessarily care for, the superficial way of experiencing foreign countries, seasickness... and you realize this is not a marriage made in heaven after all.

What you've gained, I hope, from going through this process of self-discovery, is seeing that life falls into place around doing what you love to do.

I liken it to being like a firefly. If you could blink on and off the things you 'have to' do with those which lighten your soul, imagine how serene you would feel. That peace and joy would communicate itself to others. You would attract playfulness and beauty, because you're living with playfulness and beauty.

Yes, that would be a way to live: To do all the things you need to do as though you were a firefly in June.

Improvise: *Rewrite your story*

When I'm teaching a creative writing class the lesson I repeat over and over is this: *There is no such thing as writing. There is only rewriting.*

Rewrite your story. Edit it. Polish it. Add a chapter. Put in a fuller description there, and take out a character who no longer serves you.

Reread your story, and revise it again.

You can make it even better. You can make it richer, deeper, more expressive, more thrilling or serene, more dramatic, more imbued with love and beauty...

Listen—to your authentic self. You are the only person who can write the story you want to live.

> *let yourself be truly drawn*
> *by what you truly love*
> *it will not lead you astray*
>
> —Rumi

Being responsible to our lives allows us to participate fully as co-creators.
Our freedom comes when we are able to truly respond to our life
with awareness of life, and to open our hearts, to be love. Love is
our nature, our birthright. –Diane Mariechild

Blessings on your journey

I've come a long way on my own journey, undergoing many transmutations and transformations. I've died little and big deaths all the way along.

I know you have as well.

This is what I know now from my own journey: being in love with the world, with another human being, and—hardest of all—with yourself takes a lot of practice.

But essentially this journey has brought you to a place in your soul that has to do with "love." Love is the essential nature of all creatures and things. It permeates our substance—it permeates the substance of the stars and the sky and the earth. The alchemist believes that all substance is inter-connected; I will go further than that. All substance is inter-connected and permeated with love.

This inter-connectedness brings us to a sublime understanding that is beyond the dualistic Western understanding of life, where we are trying to make sense of something entirely outside ourselves but still in relation to us.

It means we are integrated with it, and at the same time we are conscious of it.

The Sufis believe that we are born for the purpose of helping God see himself—to become conscious of himself. "A strawberry cannot taste itself" and our creator's longing is to do just that.

Thus the separation, the "I and thou." A strawberry separates from itself so it can "taste" itself. Know itself. Understand itself. Become conscious of itself.

That is what we're doing as we live. We are experiencing the taste of our own lives. We are growing more conscious of it daily—we penetrate it—we experience it. The point of tasting yourself is not to judge or have an opinion about it or like it or dislike it. The point is to *live*.

People taste in all sorts of ways. If you're scientifically inclined, you'll want to know the chemical makeup of a strawberry or its nutritional value. If you're a poet you'll describe it eloquently. If you're a farmer, you'll learn about the soil in which it grows.

It doesn't really matter how you experience the consciousness of your own being. But what does matter is that you're doing it with love.

Your love for your action, your breath, the words you speak, the things you own or give away—all this permeates the world around you with love and spreads like light. Loving what you do—whether it's "nothing" or finding a cure for cancer—is the essence of living.

Because then you'll find something equally marvelous about your life: *everything around you loves you as much as you love it.* The world has fallen in love with you. You sense the tree adoring you, the roses loving you, the wind, the stars, the waves breathing with a passion that you perhaps have experienced only in your first love.

Let yourself be loved. By your family. By your friends and coworkers. By your home and town. By the stars and the moon. By your higher self—your creator—your vast spirit self.

You are the beloved.

○┯

We are all part of the world and the world is part of us. Human–Spirit–Nature: it is all one. We are woven from the same cloth.

When you have undergone the process of letting go and being reborn and only including what matters to you and seeing things in a new light, and you ask yourself what you really want to be doing, this is your answer: do what you love. Follow your heart.

But there's more to it than that, because not only do you have to train yourself to listen to your heart and then have the courage to be guided by it, in spite of outward pressures, but there's a listening to your heart of a deeper sort.

Ultimately, you need to listen to what the world wants from you and go to meet it. You want to love the world and the people in it. You want to give to the world and the people in it. And you also want to allow it to love you. What is the world saying to you—in that strange clear passionate but steady voice my grandmother used to call "letting the forest think through you"?

It's letting the forest love you.

You are your world's lover. Yes, your world is right there, waiting and eager to love you. To be there for you. To inspire you with passion, kindness, deliberation, pleasure, and work. It's all right there in your life, in the life of your world, and it's spiraling out from you and into you.

⚏

The trees want to love you—let them. The stones. The stream. The bus driver. The sunshine. Your spouse. Your children. Your house. The roses. The neighbor. The dawn. The city. The crickets.

The bullfrogs on a long June night.

A shooting star.

You are able to commit to this love. Accept it.

All the world asks of you is to commit to it. Will you cherish it? And will you let yourself be cherished by it?

Will you let your life love you?

Say "I do."

Since beginning my own journey, I've been able to hear my heart beat in unison with the waves and the wind in the pines and I've heard the forest speak through me for the first time.

Now when I bathe it's because I know the water loves me and it inspires love in me.

Every breath I take and give is a like a whisper, and the air says a quiet "Thank you" in return.

> *"...and the end of all our exploring will be to arrive*
> *at the place and know it for the first time."*
> —*T.S. Eliot*

Suggested Additional Reading and Links

Aesop, *Aesop's Fables*

Almaas, A.H., *Diamond Heart* (series)

Anonymous, *Meditations on the Tarot*

Aurelius, Marcus, *Meditations*

Barnstone, Tony and Chou Ping, *The Anchor Book of Chinese Poetry: From Ancient to Contemporary, The Full 3000-Year Tradition*

Bausch, William J., *Storytelling: Imagination and Faith*

Blake, William, *The Marriage of Heaven and Hell*

Byrne, Rhonda, *The Secret*

Cameron, Julia, *The Artist's Way*

Chodron, Pema, *When Things Fall Apart: Heart Advice for Difficult Times*

Chopra, Deepak, *The Seven Spiritual Laws of Success: A Practical Guide to the Fulfillment of Your Dreams*

Collette, *Gigi*

Cousineau, Phil, *The Art of Forgiveness*

De Chardin, Teilhard, *Hymn to the Universe*

de Saint-Exupéry, Antoine, *Flight to Arras*

de Saint-Exupéry, Antoine, *Le Petit Prince*

Dickens, Charles, *A Christmas Carol*

Easwaran, Eknath, *Gandhi the Man: How One Man Changed Himself to Change the World*

Eliot, T.S., *The Four Quartets*

Estés, Clarissa Pinkola, *Women Who Run With Wolves*

Fallon, Bernie, *Goodology – Personal Development Through Good*

Finser, Siegfried E., *Money Can Heal*

Frankl, Viktor, *Man's Search for Meaning*

Fromm, Erich, *To Have or to Be?*

Gibran, Kahlil, *The Collected Works*

Greene, Liz, *A New Look at an Old Devil*

Greene, Liz, *The Astrology of Fate*

Hafiz, tr. Daniel James Ladinsky, *I Heard God Laughing*

Hall, Manly, *The Secret Teachings of All Ages*

Hanh, Thich Nhat, *Peace Is Every Step – The Path of Mindfulness in Everyday Life*

Hanh, Thich Nhat, *The Heart of the Buddha's Teaching: Transforming Suffering into Peace, Joy, and Liberation*
Henry David Thoreau, *Walden*
Hite, Sheilaa, *The Infinite Tarot*
Hite, Sheilaa, *The Spiritual Hedonist*
Hoffman, Enid, *Huna – A Beginner's Guide*
Jeffers, Susan, *Feel the Fear and Do it Anyway*
Jung, C.G., *Man and His Symbols*
Jung, C.G., *Structure of the Psyche*
Khoury-Ghata, Vénus, *"Les Mots" in She Says*
Klocek, Dennis, *The Seer's Handbook*
Kurz, Susan West, *Awakening Beauty*
Lax, Robert, *Love had a Compass – Journals and Poetry*
Pollan, Michael, *The Botany of Desire*
Lerner, Harriet, *The Dance of Anger*
Long, Maxwell Freedom, *Growing into Light*
Long, Maxwell Freedom, *Recovering the Ancient Magic*
Maraboli, Steve, *Life, the Truth, and Being Free*
Mariechild, Diane, *MotherWit–A Guide to Healing & Psychic Development*
Markovia, Dawna, *I Will Not Die an Unlived Life*
Matthews, Caitlin, *Singing the Soul Back Home*
McKee, Robert, *Story*
Morrell, Rima A, *The Secret Power of Huna*
Moss, Robert, *Conscious Dreaming: A Spiritual Path for Everyday Life*
Nin, Anais, *The Diary of Anais Nin*
O'Neill, JP, ed., *Unstruck Music: Spiritual Poetry by Kabir*
Pilgrim, Peace, *Steps Toward Inner Peace*
Place, Robert M., *Alchemy and the Tarot*
Porter, Eliot, *In Wildness Is the Preservation of the World*
Prior, James Lane (Pama Rab Sel), *The Divine Moment*
Pukui, Mary Kawena, *'Olelo No'eau: Hawaiian Proverbs and Poetical Sayings*
Pukui, Mary Kawena and E.W. Haertig, *Nana i Ke Kumu (Look to the Source)*
Rinpoche, Sogyal, *The Tibetan Book of Living and Dying*
Robbins, Tom, *Another Roadside Attraction*
Rumi, Jalal al-Din Rumi, *The Essential Rumi*

Sambhava, Padma, compiler, Robert Thurman, tr., *The Tibetan Book of the Dead: The Great Book of Natural Liberation Through Understanding in the Between*

Shedd, John Augustus, *Salt from My Attic*

Silverstein, Shel, *Falling Up*

St. John of the Cross, *Dark Night of the Soul*

Steiner, Rudolf, *Knowledge of the Higher Worlds*

Steiner, Rudolf, *Philosophy of Freedom*

Tolle, Eckhart, *The Power of Now: A Guide to Spiritual Enlightenment*

Tulku, Ringu, *Daring Steps: Traversing The Path Of The Buddha*

Tyler, Anne, *The Accidental Tourist*

Waggoner, Diane, *The Beauty of Life: William Morris & the Art of Design*

Walsch, Neal Donald, *Conversations with God*

Watts, Alan, *The Way of Zen*

Watts, Alan, *Become Who You Are*

Watts, Alan, *The Wisdom of Insecurity*

Williamson, Marianne, *A Return to Love: Reflections on the Principles of A Course in Miracles*

Wolters, Clifton, tr., *The Cloud of Unknowing*

Yogananda, Paramahansa, *Inner Peace – How to Be Calmly Active and Actively Calm*

Zambucka, Kristin, *The Fire Lily (Ka Lilia O Ke Ahi)*

Nicholson, Sarah, *http://sarahsphotographs.com/*

Interview with Toni Morrison from *The Guardian* (April 13, 2012) http://www.guardian.co.uk/books/2012/apr/13/toni-morrison-home-son-love

Dalai Lama quoted from his *Nobel Prize winning lecture*: http://www.dalailama.com/messages/acceptance-speeches/nobel-peace-prize/nobel-lecture

Paul Newman quoted on his *imdb site*: http://www.imdb.com/name/nm0000056/bio

Stephen Fry quoted in an article in *The Guardian*, Tuesday 20 July 2010 http://www.guardian.co.uk/media/2010/jul/20/stephen-fry-bbc-planet-word

Author's website: winsloweliot.com
Publisher's website: writespa.com
Web developer's website: promoteglobally.com
Cover designer's website: jasperlark.com

You are the sky. Everything else—it's just the weather. —Pema Chödrön

Winslow Eliot is a writing coach, mentor, and editor. She wrote her first novel in 1983 and since then eight more novels have been published in over twenty countries and translated into eleven languages. Her online *"WriteSpa – An Oasis for People Who Love to Write"* welcomes visitors from all over the world. Her series on rejuvenating other people's pleasure in writing, called *Writing through the Year,* is also available.

Her novels include *Pursued, Heaven Falls, A Perfect Gem, The Happiness Cure,* and *Bright Face of Danger.*

Other books she's written:
Illustrated Atlas of Native American History, ed. Samuel W. Crompton. Contrib. Author: *Accommodation, Exchange, and Warfare 1600 – 1700; The Waldorf Book of Breads;* and a collection of poems called *Poems from the Oasis.*

Besides writing novels and managing her WriteSpa, she teaches high school (creative writing, literature and history seminars, and English). She also belly-dances, sings and plays guitar, and she has visited many sacred places in the world. She continues to study with and learn from her fellow seekers, her teachers, and her students.

CPSIA information can be obtained at www.ICGtesting.com
Printed in the USA
BVOW080949011212

307026BV00002B/25/P